Praise for *Field Guide for Small Group Leaders*

"Whether we are first-time small group leaders or seasoned disciple-makers, we all need some guidance and direction along the way. Sam O'Neal has walked the path of small groups and now serves as a tour guide for those who wish to join in the adventure of leadership. With practical tips and refreshing honesty, O'Neal gives step-by-step direction for establishing a healthy and transformational community, warns of potential pitfalls and offers encouragement for many of the common challenges that leaders face."

HEATHER ZEMPEL, author of *Sacred Roads* and *Community Is Messy*

"Small groups often struggle, so we need a trusted guide on how to improve them. Sam O'Neal is my guide of choice, because he's not only read the literature on small groups, he has lived his life in them."

KEVIN MILLER, associate rector, Church of the Resurrection, Wheaton, IL

"With the dizzying array of methods and models for small groups out there, who couldn't use a little help navigating the landscape? I can't think of a better guide than Sam O'Neal. Sam knows small groups. He's participated in them, led them and studied them. *Field Guide for Small Group Leaders* is the perfect primer on the subject. With clean, engaging prose, Sam clears the fog surrounding the topic and delivers advice for small group leaders that is both practical and biblical. Pastors, make sure your small group leaders don't head into their next meetings without this valuable resource in hand."

DREW DYCK, managing editor of *Leadership Journal* and author of *Generation Ex-Christian*

"I've always felt that leading a small group is more art than science, more organic than mechanical. But you can't ignore the mechanics, and even art has underlying tips and techniques, which, if mastered, enhance the authenticity of the medium. Samuel O'Neal's *Field Guide for Small Group Leaders* provides many such techniques as practiced by a master artist. His application of learning styles alone has already improved my own group leadership."

DAVE TREAT, small group consultant and trainer, thingingsmall.net

Field Guide for
Small Group
Leaders

Sam O'Neal

Peter & Miriam Co
610-88A Street SW
Edmonton, Alberta, Canada
T6X 1C3

IVP Connect
An imprint of InterVarsity Press
Downers Grove, Illinois

InterVarsity Press
P.O. Box 1400, Downers Grove, IL 60515-1426
World Wide Web: www.ivpress.com
E-mail: email@ivpress.com

InterVarsity Press® is the book-publishing division of InterVarsity Christian Fellowship/USA®, a movement of students and faculty active on campus at hundreds of universities, colleges and schools of nursing in the United States of America, and a member movement of the International Fellowship of Evangelical Students. For information about local and regional activities, write Public Relations Dept., InterVarsity Christian Fellowship/USA, 6400 Schroeder Rd., P.O. Box 7895, Madison, WI 53707-7895, or visit the IVCF website at <www.intervarsity.org>.

All Scripture quotations, unless otherwise indicated, are taken from the Holy Bible, New International Version®. NIV®. Copyright ©1973, 1978, 1984 by International Bible Society. Used by permission of Zondervan Publishing House. All rights reserved.

While all stories in this book are true, some names and identifying information in this book have been changed to protect the privacy of the individuals involved.

Cover design: Cindy Kiple
Interior design: Beth Hagenberg
Images: Visual Mozart/Getty Images

ISBN 978-0-8308-1091-8

Printed in the United States of America ∞

Library of Congress Cataloging-in-Publication Data

O'Neal, Sam, 1981-
    Field guide for small group leaders: setting the tone,
accommodating learning styles, and more/Sam O'Neal.
        p. cm.
    Includes bibliographical references.
    ISBN 978-0-8308-1091-8 (pbk.: alk. paper)
    1. Church group work. 2. Small groups. 3. Christian leadership.
I. Title.
    BV652.2. O54 2012
    253'.7—dc23

2012000257

P	18	17	16	15	14	13	12	11	10	9	8	7	6	5	4	3	2	1
Y	27	26	25	24	23	22	21	20	19	18	17	16	15	14	13	12		

For my Angel Lewa.
You are my greatest treasure,
my hightest motivation
and my best friend.

Contents

Introduction

The happiest moment of my life took place during a small group gathering.

It was October 13, 2002. I had finished my undergraduate work a few months earlier and was living in a house with five of my best friends from school. I was also deeply in love with a beautiful young woman named Jessica, and—on that crisp day in Wheaton, Illinois—I was getting ready to ask for her hand in marriage.

The two of us had spent the afternoon retracing some of our favorite haunts and reliving some of our favorite memories. When we arrived back at the house, all five of my buddies were there to greet us. They were watching a baseball game, I think.

When the guys left the room at my signal, I grabbed my guitar from its hiding place behind the TV and played a song that ended with the words "Will you be my wife?" Then I got down on one knee and pulled the ring out from underneath the couch where she was sitting. I heard a couple of the guys snickering in the hall when Jess pinned my arms to my chest with a hug so that I had trouble getting the ring on her finger. But then all five of them were cheering and high-fiving each other. Before long, they were praying for my fiancée and me—pouring blessings over us and beseeching God to unite us in the strongest bonds of love. And then we brought out food and drinks and celebrated together for hours.

Maybe you don't see the appeal in having a group of guys hanging around and gawking at you during one of the more personal moments of your life. That's okay. I get that.

But for me, inviting my friends to participate in that happiest of moments was natural. It was instinctive. That's because the six of us had become more than ordinary friends. We were more like brothers—young men on the cusp of adulthood, all connected at a deeper level by a shared experience of authentic Christian community.

My Story

Growing up, I was unfailingly attracted to superficial expressions of community: sports teams, academic clubs, youth groups and so on. I enjoyed connecting with others through shared experiences, and I liked the idea of having friends—to a point. With very few exceptions, I preferred to keep relationships at a superficial level instead of looking for ways to go deeper.

That's why living in a house with five of my closest friends was a transformational experience for me—and I try not to use that word lightly. That year was a turning point that changed my life.

Sure, in many ways we were a typical group of young, irresponsible guys still unsure of what it meant to live in the "real world." We spent a lot of time watching movies and playing video games. We didn't sleep much, usually because intense games of Monopoly demanded our attention into the early hours of the morning. We made fun of each other and played jokes on each other and shared a lot of frozen dinners.

But we also prayed for each other regularly and intensely. We gathered for shared devotions many times throughout the week—

sometimes scheduled, but often spontaneous. Several of us played guitar (at several different skill levels), and people often heard the sound of our worship from the sidewalks outside. We confessed our sins to each other, we repented, and we requested account- ability for that repentance because we wanted to become better men. Even more, we invited freshmen and sophomores from the school to participate in these activities with us; we tried to serve as mentors to the best of our ability.

In short, although we didn't realize it at the time, our house began to resemble the kind of community highlighted in Acts 2:42-47.

> They devoted themselves to the apostles' teaching and to the fellowship, to the breaking of bread and to prayer. Everyone was filled with awe, and many wonders and miraculous signs were done by the apostles. All the believers were together and had everything in common. Selling their possessions and goods, they gave to anyone as he had need. Every day they continued to meet together in the temple courts. They broke bread in their homes and ate together with glad and sincere hearts, praising God and enjoying the favor of all the people. And the Lord added to their number daily those who were being saved.

I consider that year spent "doing life together" with friends as my first encounter with the modern phenomenon known as "small groups." In many ways it was the best small group I've ever expe- rienced; it was certainly the most intense. And when it ended, I wanted more.

Fortunately, Jess and I were invited to participate in our church's small group for young couples after we were engaged. When the group leader and his wife moved to a different state several months after our wedding, Jess and I took his place.

That was my first official post as a small group leader, and the results were mixed. Yes, our group provided a place for young

couples to build relationships and eventually put down roots
within the broader congregation. Yes, many of us grew in our
knowledge and understanding of God's Word. Yes, we learned a
great deal about our spouses. (Incidentally, for these reasons and
more my wife and I have continued to lead a young couples small
group every year we've been married.)

At the same time, these positive gains were continually derailed
by a wide variety of distractions, including relational conflict and
mistrust. The group suffered from a lack of direction—were we
meeting every week to learn about the Bible? To form relationships? To pray? To become better wives and husbands? I don't
think any of us were sure.

Worst of all, the members of the group (myself included) were
experiencing very little in the way of spiritual transformation.
Certainly, when I compared the results of that group to the year I
had spent living in a true version of Christian community, I felt
like a failure.

Looking back on that experience after almost a decade of leading small groups, what galls me most is that I could have solved
the problems that kept knocking us off track if I had been properly trained, or if I had taken the time to seek the advice of those
more experienced in small group ministry.

Thankfully, it wasn't long before I got a boost in my small group
education.

I first accepted a job with Christianity Today in the summer of
2005, just a few months after my wife and I moved away from our
first church and first small group. I was the assistant editor for
PreachingToday.com, and I enjoyed the work immensely. (That's
because I spent most of my time editing and outlining sermons
written by some of the most accomplished preachers in the
world—not a bad gig.)

But then, during a weekly staff meeting at the beginning of
2007, I experienced another life-changing moment when our vice

president announced: "We are finalizing a contract to purchase a website called SmallGroups.com. We'll need an editor to run the site, so let me know if there's anyone you'd like to recommend."

I certainly had someone to recommend! I was still involved with small groups—still fascinated by their potential as a source for transformational community. At the same time, I remembered the failures of my first experience attempting to lead such a community.

Therefore, when I accepted the position of managing editor for SmallGroups.com, my twofold mission was clear:

1. to learn all I could about successfully leading a small group

2. to use SmallGroups.com as a platform to distribute what I learned to churches and small group leaders around the world

I had the privilege of working on those two goals for more than five years, and I'm pleased with the results.

I learned a ton, for one thing. SmallGroups.com contains archived content that goes all the way back to 1996, and I had the opportunity to read every page of it. Even more, I was blessed to work with many of the leading authorities on small group ministry from across the country—dozens of men and women, pastors and laypersons, who have contributed toward SmalGroups.com's mission of "inspiring life-changing community."

I'm also more than pleased with the way SmallGroups.com has impacted churches, groups and individuals around the world. It's a great feeling to attend conferences or meet with churches and hear from people in the trenches of small group ministry that they have appreciated our efforts.

At the end of 2011 I accepted a position with Lifeway Christian Resources as an editor for books and Bible studies written for young adults—another fascinating continuation of my education. Fortunately, I remain an editorial advisor for SmallGroups.com, which means I can now contribute to (and benefit from) the world of small groups on two fronts.

My Goals for This Book

Which brings me to why I've written this book. On the one hand, this book is an extension of the two goals I adopted for Small Groups.com. Writing and revising this manuscript has certainly been a learning process—a great way for me to define and sharpen my own beliefs about small groups. And it is my sincere hope that this book reaches a number of new and established small group leaders who, like me all those years ago, could use a bit of training and direction.

On the other hand, I am attempting through these pages to focus on one specific element of small group ministry: a group leader's responsibility to prepare for and lead small group meetings.

To me, this responsibility is the keystone of a small group ministry. If group leaders can be successful in this task, their groups have an excellent chance of developing into spiritually healthy communities. And if groups are healthy, the small group ministry as a whole will be full of life. And if a church's small group ministry is thriving, the church will have a greater impact for the kingdom of God within the community. And on it goes.

So, if you are a small group leader, I believe your efforts at planning and leading your group week after week and month after month are of great importance. And I sincerely hope this book will help.

I don't say this book will make things easy for you, all of a sudden. In order to prepare for and lead a small group meeting, you will need to act as a semiexpert in theology, discipleship, Christian education, worship, prayer, interpersonal dynamics and more. And that will never be "easy as 1-2-3."

But my goal in writing this book is to make that process a bit easier. I want to make sure your foundation as a leader is secure, and I want to equip you with a few tools (some basic, others more advanced) that will serve you as you go about your work.

One more thing, and this is not really a goal as much as a

request from me to you. The core idea behind this ministry we call "small groups" is that disciples of Jesus are not meant to follow after him alone. God is a divine community, and we are made in his image—created to live and learn and love and serve in community as well.

So here's my request: don't read this book alone if you can help it. Don't attempt to train yourself in how to lead a small group as if this were a textbook and you have a quiz tomorrow morning.

Rather, read this book in community with others. Read it with a mentor who has experience leading groups and can help you process what you learn. Read it with fellow group leaders who will be preparing for and leading small group meetings alongside you. Talk about what you find within these pages. Discuss what you find helpful or confusing or just plain weird.

That's my request, anyway. Thank you for reading, and may God bless your faithful service.

PART ONE

Mapping the Terrain

If you've ever been to Walt Disney World, you know it's a great place for family fun. You also know that it's really, really big—the developed section of the park alone takes up about ten thousand acres. That much space provides room for four theme parks, two water parks, six golf courses, thirty-six hotels, over one hundred restaurants, and an entire transportation system complete with highways, monorails and canals. Whew!

Of course, that much space can also be a nightmare when it comes to navigation.

Disney provides two different tools to help visitors get around quickly and safely. The first is a detailed series of printed maps. These maps show everything, right down to the restrooms and Lemon Ice vendors. But I find them to be less than helpful. For one thing, you need an engineering degree to refold the things after they've been opened. More importantly, the maps don't give you any perspective. They show you everything in the park that can be visited, but it takes a complex series of identifying landmarks and triangulating distances before you can figure out where you actually are.

That's why I prefer Disney's second navigational tool: the directories. These are free-standing kiosks spread throughout the park that display larger versions of the printed maps, but with one critical difference: each directory contains a red arrow with the words "You are here." Armed with the knowledge of where you are on the map, it's pretty easy to orient yourself and decide where you want to go.

That's the goal of this book's first section. Whether you are a new small group leader or a veteran of many years, I want to make sure you have a proper orientation when it comes to leading other people as part of a transformational, Christ-centered community.

To do that, the first three chapters will explore the important foundational elements of leading a small group:

- Chapter one provides answers to basic questions: What is a small group? What are the primary purpose and essential activities of a small group meeting? What is your role as "leader"?

- Chapter two explores the place of hospitality within your role as a small group leader.

- Chapter three helps you get a better understanding of your group members (and yourself) through an introduction to learning styles.

Solidifying your grasp on these concepts will give you that red arrow—it will help you understand where you are and prepare you to move forward into something exciting.

1

Small Groups 101

I've got good news and bad news for any current or potential small group leaders reading this book.

First, the good news: It's rare for people to have a totally negative experience during a small group gathering. Bad things do happen on occasion, of course. But it's unlikely that you will ever lead an unmitigated disaster of a group meeting—one where the majority of participants feel angry or cheated or wronged. I base that statement on ten years of personal experience with small group gatherings, plus hundreds of conversations with group leaders and participants.

Think about it: small groups offer a chance for social interaction and relationships within a collection of nice people (generally speaking) in a culture where 25 percent of the population lacks even one close friend.[1] Even more, small groups are a venue for exploring the Bible—the bestselling book of all time—and its intersection with the troubles and triumphs of everyday life.

Sometimes you even get free food!

Now the bad news: Even though it's uncommon for people to have a terrible experience during a small group gathering, it's just as rare for group members to experience something that is overwhelmingly positive—something that moves beyond the realm of polite get-togethers and surface conversations, and justifies the continual investment of time and effort required by the leader and participants alike.

In other words, most people who participate in a small group don't see their lives changed because of it. They don't experience transformation.

Again, I know this because I've heard the stories. As we were rebuilding SmallGroups.com, throughout our conversations with pastors and group leaders, one theme kept popping up again and again: "We like the idea of small groups, and we understand the basic format—but how do we get them to actually work?"

That's the question I will be tackling throughout this book. But first I need to narrow the focus a little bit.

Small Group Meetings and Spiritual Growth

If I've learned anything from my family in recent years, it's that the word *mother* is a complicated, multilayered title with many applications. My wife is the primary nurturer of our children, for example, but she is also their principal educator. And their chauffer. And their chef. And their personal trainer. And their doctor. And on and on it goes.

There's a similar dynamic at play when it comes to small group leaders in the Western church. Depending on your church's denomination or model of small group ministry, you may be asked to perform several (or even all) of the following tasks: recruiting group members, training an apprentice, tracking birthdays and anniversaries, arranging childcare, filing attendance reports, mentoring potential group leaders, planning social events and more.

All of those tasks are important, and each of them can contribute to the overall health of a small group—I want to be clear about that. But those tasks are not the focus of this book, and I won't offer much advice about them in these pages.

There are two reasons for this. First, because it's usually best for small group leaders to delegate some or even all of those tasks to an apprentice or to other members of the group. Doing so relieves some of the pressure felt by the group leader and empowers other participants to take ownership within the group, which moves them to a deeper level of commitment.

Second, I won't spend a lot of time on the secondary tasks of small group leadership because there are several resources that already provide helpful guidance for completing those tasks—especially SmallGroups.com. In fact, appendix one at the back of this book lists the best articles and downloadable resources from SmallGroups.com that cover topics and tasks not directly addressed in these pages.

So, what is the focus of this book? Put simply, I want to help small group leaders prepare for and lead transformational small group meetings (or gatherings or whatever you call them). I want to equip group leaders with ideas and tools that will help them maximize that hour or two spent with group members—and the chain of group meetings as they occur over weeks and months—in such a way that spiritual growth occurs and participants' lives are changed for the better.

In other words, I want your small group to work.

Each chapter in this book will help you take a specific step toward that goal. For the remaining pages in this chapter, however, I think it's important to lay out some basic definitions and answer some foundational questions.

What Is a Small Group?

I mentioned earlier that there are several different methods and models of small group ministry, which means there is no real consensus on the definition of a small group. The SmallGroups.com team developed the following definition of a small group as we were laying the foundations for the site, and I think it fits well for the purposes of this book:

A small group is a collection of between three and thirty people who regularly meet and participate in activities together with the goal of experiencing spiritual growth.

There are a number of key terms that need to be highlighted here. First, we limited a small group to "between three and thirty people." Our team chose the lower number because three people (rather than an individual or a pair) is the smallest number that can be considered a group. The upper number was harder to define. Many small group practitioners believe that an ideal group contains six to ten people.[2] However, it is possible to deal with larger numbers by "subgrouping" (dividing the group into smaller subgroups for discussion, prayer or other activities). At the same time, growing beyond thirty people pushes the boundaries on practical matters like finding enough chairs for everyone, parking and maintaining relationships.

Next, it's important that a small group be defined as a collection of people who "regularly meet." Most groups meet once every week, although there are a number of groups that remain healthy while gathering every two weeks or even once a month. This regular interaction is a key ingredient in the formation of what we often refer to as "community"—that state of being where a group of people form deeper relationships through regular interaction and a common purpose.

As the author of Hebrews writes: "Let us consider how we may spur one another on toward love and good deeds. Let us not give up meeting together, as some are in the habit of doing, but let us encouraging one another—and all the more as you see the Day approaching" (Hebrews 10:24-25). In my opinion it would be difficult for a group to maintain cohesion if the participants gather together less frequently than once a month—or if they meet sporadically, without a regular schedule and defined intervals between each gathering.

Finally, members of a small group "participate in activities together with the goal of experiencing spiritual growth." People need to do stuff when they get together as a group—they need to take part in specific activities. And the ultimate goal of those activities is to help group members mature and develop as disciples of Jesus Christ. On the other side, those activities also help group members reject sin and elements of the world that would drag them away from Jesus Christ (and thus limit their spiritual growth).

This echoes Peter's words to the early church: "Therefore, dear friends, since you already know this, be on your guard so that you may not be carried away by the error of lawless men and fall from your secure position. But grow in the grace and knowledge of our Lord and Savior Jesus Christ. To him be glory both now and forever! Amen" (2 Peter 3:17-18).

What Is the Primary Purpose of a Small Group Meeting?

I briefly answered this earlier, but it's worth a bit of further exploration. The goal of a small group is spiritual growth. It's transformation. It's helping participants move away from that first gasping breath they took as born-again children of God, still wallowing in their sin, and toward their ultimate identity as fully glorified disciples of Christ. (And, if your group has evangelistic success, it's seeing participants take that first breath as newly born children of God.)

Maybe you're thinking, *Isn't spiritual growth the goal of each Chris-*

tian as an individual? Yes it is. Anyone who follows Jesus as their Lord is supposed to be working toward becoming more like him every day (see John 13:12-17). We have a lot of words for that process—*sanctification, spiritual growth, transformation, life change* and so on.

The thing is, when I look back over my life, I see the least amount of spiritual growth during those times when I tried to go it alone. Just recently, for example, I had the chance to supervise the revision of a major study Bible. It was a freelance assignment, which meant I did most of my work during evenings and weekends. I spent a full year in verse-by-verse exploration of the Bible, and as part of the editing process I read through and evaluated all seven thousand study notes—twice.

By the end of the project I was a little sick of Bible verses, to be honest. And I had real trouble getting motivated to interpret and discuss portions of Scripture with my small group (let alone leading the process). So I withdrew. I pulled back from my group members. I didn't quit the group or anything, but I isolated myself both inside and outside our group meetings. And I encountered consequences because of that isolation—damage to myself spiritually and damage to the progress of our group.

I like what Kevin Miller (a former vice president of Christianity Today) used to say during our planning meetings: "Spiritual growth never happens in a vacuum."

I also like how Paul highlights this idea in Ephesians 4, starting with verses 1-7:

> As a prisoner for the Lord, then, I urge you to live a life worthy of the calling you have received. Be completely humble and gentle; be patient, bearing with one another in love. Make every effort to keep the unity of the Spirit through the bond of peace. There is one body and one Spirit—just as you were called to one hope when you were called—one Lord, one faith, one baptism; one God and Fa-

ther of all, who is over all and through all and in all.

But to each one of us grace has been given as Christ apportioned it.

After a little tangent regarding Christ's resurrection and ascension, Paul continues with verses 11-16:

It was he who gave some to be apostles, some to be prophets, some to be evangelists, and some to be pastors and teachers, to prepare God's people for works of service, so that the body of Christ may be built up until we all reach unity in the faith and in the knowledge of the Son of God and become mature, attaining to the whole measure of the fullness of Christ.

Then we will no longer be infants, tossed back and forth by the waves, and blown here and there by every wind of teaching and by the cunning and craftiness of men in their deceitful scheming. Instead, speaking the truth in love, we will in all things grow up into him who is the Head, that is, Christ. From him the whole body, joined and held together by every supporting ligament, grows and builds itself up in love, as each part does its work.

Notice how the individual and communal elements of the Christian life are interwoven throughout the passage. Christ gives grace to "each one of us" so that "the body of Christ may be built up" and we all "become mature, attaining to the whole measure of the fullness of Christ." Individual Christians use their callings as apostles, teachers and so on in order that "we will in all things grow up into him who is the Head, that is, Christ."

Personal sanctification is important, yes, but our growth in Christ as individuals is supplemented and boosted when we choose to work toward that goal as part of a community. This communal desire for spiritual growth is the primary purpose of your small group as a whole, and it should be the primary goal of each individual small group meeting you lead.

What Are the Essential Activities of a Small Group Meeting?

So, what happens in a small group that helps people achieve that primary goal of spiritual growth and transformation? The following is a list of what I consider to be the core practices the participants of a group should undertake when they gather together—the essential activities or elements of a small group meeting.

Social connection and fellowship. Small group members need time to hang out and enjoy each other's company. Doing so helps everyone form and maintain strong relationships, and it is the relational nature of small groups that separates it from personal spiritual growth (devotions) and corporate events (weekend worship services). Social interaction can (and should) happen outside of group meetings, as well.

Interaction with God's Word. I don't think small groups should avoid topical discussions, or that every group meeting needs to be a straight-out Bible study. However, I do believe the Bible needs to be the primary source of truth for a small group, and that source needs to be accessed and examined habitually. In Jesus' words: "If you hold to my teaching, you are really my disciples. Then you will know the truth, and the truth will set you free" (John 8:31-32). Otherwise a small group devolves into a Kiwanis Club or group therapy at a psychologist's office.

Group discussion. The exchange of ideas is an important element within a small group—sharing opinions, asking questions, sharing interpretations, expressing confusion and so on. (This includes discussion about the Bible, but also other topics and ideas.) Without this "iron sharpens iron" aspect, a small group becomes a lecture in a classroom.

Learning activities. Learning activities is a broad term, but I use it in reference to the educational elements of a group meeting that go beyond discussion. This includes icebreakers, object lessons, role plays and so on. These elements are important because they appeal to group members with various learning styles and preferences.

Prayer. Approaching God through prayer has always been a core practice of Jesus' disciples, both as individuals and corporately. Indeed, the New Testament is bursting with commands about prayer written to the members of the early church. "Do not be anxious about anything, but in everything, by prayer and petition, with thanksgiving, present your requests to God" is a good example (Philippians 4:6). So is 1 Thessalonians 5:16-18: "Be joyful always; pray continually; give thanks in all circumstances, for this is God's will for you in Christ Jesus."

Worship. Worship is an appropriate response to our interaction with God and his Word during a small group meeting. And it should be noted that worship in a small group can incorporate music and singing—but it doesn't have to. Other expressions of worship include contemplation, *lectio divina*, Scripture reading, liturgical prayer, physical movement and more.

Application. I like what Eugene Peterson writes about applying God's Word: "The most important question we ask of any text isn't 'What does this mean?' but 'What can I obey?' Simple obedience will open up our lives to a text more than any number of Bible studies, dictionaries, and concordances."[3] The best group meetings include interacting with and discussing God's Word, but they don't stop there—they move toward application. Sometimes this means discussing how group members can apply lessons learned in their individual lives, and other times this involves group members getting off their seats and taking action together.

Again, this list is based on my personal experience, but also on my interaction with small group practitioners on SmallGroups .com. The articles and resources we put together on the topics listed here are consistently the most accessed and appreciated by our readers.

One more thing: It's important to note that group leaders don't have to shoehorn all of these activities into every one of their small group meetings—nor do they have to make sure that each element receives equal time. It's appropriate to spend a group meeting entirely in prayer, for example (or discussion, application, fellowship and so on). It would also be appropriate to defer worship and learning activities if a group member required an extended time of prayer.

What Is Your Primary Role as a Small Group Leader?

If the purpose of a small group (and small group meetings) is spiritual growth for everyone participating, how does the group leader fit into that process? How do we lead other people in a way that results in spiritual transformation?

Those are important questions. Unfortunately, I believe they have been answered incorrectly by a lot of pastors and ministry directors. As a result, a large percentage of small group leaders in the Western church are suffering from an identity crisis.

Here's a quick question to show you what I mean: What label does your church currently use to describe your ministry role? Are you a small group leader? A host? A facilitator? A shepherd? Are you part of a life group, a home group, a connection group, a community group—or something completely different? I've encountered each of these terms over the years, and I usually see a new one on a church website every few months.

On the one hand, it's not a big deal that different churches use different terminology to describe the same ministry role. People have diverse ways of expressing themselves. Church leaders emphasize one word over another as a way of prioritizing specific functions or tasks. It's to be expected.

On the other hand, I think this wide variety of ministry titles can be viewed as a symptom of the larger identity crisis affecting small group ministries today. Put simply, many group leaders in today's churches don't have a firm grasp on what their role is supposed to be, which means they don't have a firm grasp on the goals they are trying to accomplish, which means they don't have a firm grasp at all about what they are supposed to be doing in their groups.

This identity crisis manifests itself in two ways:

1. *Small group leaders suffer from a lack of focus.* When group leaders don't have a clear focus regarding their ministry role, they often wander. They become like ships without a rudder, drifting from one current to the next.

   That's a bad thing for group leaders and group members alike. When people attempt to lead others without clarity and confidence, the result is a hesitant exploration of truth and stunted spiritual formation for all involved—and that's the best-case scenario. At worst, group leaders suffering from a lack of focus can unwittingly pilot their groups toward heresy, apathy, bitterness or a destructive combination of all three.

2. *Small group leaders suffer from a misguided focus.* Many small group leaders have an idea about their ministry role that is both practical and well-defined—but also inaccurate. In other words, they have a strong focus, but they are pointed in the wrong direction. This can happen when a church actively points its group leaders the wrong way, or when group leaders choose their own focus after drifting for a while in the already-mentioned scenario.

   This second manifestation of the identity crisis is especially damaging because it is so subtle and insidious. It is entirely possible for you as a small group leader to genuinely care for the people in your group, to be dedicated in your ministry role, to research all the latest tips about group dynamics and interpersonal relationships—and yet to lead your group gatherings in a way that results in little or no spiritual fruit. And all because you were pointed in the wrong direction from the beginning.

So let me take a minute to identify several of the "wrong directions" that are common in small group ministries today. Generally speaking, a small group leader should not be defined *primarily* as any of the following when it comes to leading others during group meetings:

Teacher. You've probably encountered a "lecturer" in a small group before, whether it was the group leader or a member. This is someone who monopolizes everyone's time by spewing out facts and opinions one after another. And that's a bad idea. We know that.

But I use the word *teacher* here intentionally in order to highlight an important misconception: many group leaders believe that their primary role is that of a teacher. They feel the group is successful if the people involved are learning facts and ideas about God, the Bible and the world—especially if people can regurgitate those facts. But that's not the case. It's possible to comprehend all kinds of spiritual doctrines and ideas, yet still remain spiritually stagnant. (Just ask the Pharisees.)

As small group leaders, we must understand that it's entirely possible to be an excellent teacher—not someone who is a "lecturer" but someone who genuinely helps people learn during group meetings—and yet still fail to help our group members become more like Jesus Christ. As Paul said: "Knowledge puffs up, but love builds up" (1 Corinthians 8:1).

Facilitator. Many churches want their group leaders to think of themselves as facilitators rather than leaders. This is done to combat the "small group leader as lecturer" problem already referred to, or to prevent people from claiming the title of *leader* and lording it over the other members of the group.

But this approach creates several problems of its own. Just as viewing group leaders primarily as teachers elevates information over transformation, viewing them as facilitators elevates discussion over transformation. The group is deemed successful if people experience good conversation and a high level of participation rather than basing the criteria for success on interaction with the Holy Spirit resulting in spiritual growth.

Host. In recent years, host has become a popular redefinition of what it means to be a small group leader, primarily due to the influence of video curriculum. The idea is that a person or couple can host a small group in their home, pop in a DVD and let a "professional" handle the task of leading the group into meaningful experiences with God and his Word.

But there is one major flaw inherent in this method of "leading" a small group: a DVD cannot respond to the movement of the Holy Spirit. A prerecorded video cannot care for people or provide targeted encouragement and support. So what happens when a group member is convicted of sin during the discussion and begins weeping? Who calls the group to prayer when a couple mentions they are in danger of losing their house or their marriage? These situations require a leader. And that leader is supposed to be you.

Another group member. There are many pastors and church leaders who don't like the term *leader.* They discourage their small group leaders from acting differently than group members because they want to communicate that group members are just as important and valuable as group leaders—which is true.

But being equal in terms of worth and value does not mean that people have to adopt the same roles and functions. The reality is that a small group with no leader will rarely move forward.

Let me be clear about one thing before moving on: I'm not saying that small group leaders should avoid demonstrating any of these important qualities. Quite the opposite—group leaders should be able to facilitate discussions, host a gathering and teach when necessary. Those are important and necessary skills. What I am saying is that group leaders go wrong when they make any of these skills the primary focus of their role within their groups.

Okay, now we're back to that important question from a couple pages ago: How do we lead a small group meeting in a way that results in spiritual growth? What is the primary role of a small group leader?

Let's start with a definition.

A small group leader prepares for small group meetings, both short-term and long-term, and leads his or her group members through the essential activities of those meetings in submission to the Holy Spirit.

First is the necessity of preparation. Group leaders are charged with scheduling the essential activities performed by the group—social interaction, discussion, prayer, worship and so on. Group leaders also perform research or acquire supplies as necessary to help the group get the most out of those activities.

This preparation occurs both in the short-term and long-term. As a group leader you will set the agenda and prepare an activity for the meeting coming up this Wednesday, but you'll also keep a loose plan in place for the five other meetings that will take place before Easter. (I'll go into greater detail on how to prepare for a small group meeting in part two.)

This next word is important: a small group leader *leads*. Simply put, you need to embrace your role as a leader within your group. That doesn't mean you are more valuable than the other group members, but it does mean that your role is set apart from theirs. When there is a need for someone in the group to make a decision, offer guidance, provide clarity or choose a direction—that person needs to be you.

More, a small group leader needs to lead "his or her group members." The people within your group are unique individuals with unique strengths, weaknesses, needs and gifts. That means you will be most effective as a leader when you tailor the elements of a group meeting to maximize those strengths and gifts—and to address those areas of weakness and need. It's also important to have an idea of how your group members are coming together as a group. They are not a collection of individuals attempting spiritual growth separately; they are a community of people growing together.

For these reasons you need to get to know your group members through genuine relationships. You cannot lead well if you remain isolated from the people following you.

The final phrase is important: "in submission to the Holy Spirit." A small group gathering is more than a collection of ordinary activities and rituals performed by people. The goal of these meetings is spiritual growth, which makes them spiritual in nature—it makes them supernatural, in fact. And that means they require the presence and impact of the Holy Spirit in order to be successful.

Now it's time for the analogy.

Small Group Leaders as Spiritual Safari Guides

Imagine the following scenario:

You are going on a safari. You've done extensive research and picked out the perfect wilderness organization to help you come face-to-face with elephants or crocodiles or monkeys or exotic birds—whatever series of animals really gets your fire going. Sure it's expensive, but this is a once-in-a-lifetime experience. You are totally excited.

You purchase tickets to Africa or South America and you have a great experience on the flight. You've packed lots of new survival clothing and high-tech wilderness gadgets, and by some miracle all your luggage arrives at the same airport as you—and at the same time. Things couldn't be going better.

Pretty soon you are riding in a Jeep with four other adventurers. Your safari guide is driving. His name is Crush, or something cool like that, and he speaks perfect English. He looks very rugged and dependable—very capable of thriving in the wild and helping others do the same. Plus, he's wearing the same kind of hat as Crocodile Dundee in that movie you really liked.

When everyone gets out of the Jeep, you are standing on the threshold of an untamed jungle. You can see huge trees full of exotic leaves and vines. You smell the light perfume of wild blossoms mixed with the musty scent of bark and leaves and dirt. You hear the bubbling of a river somewhere off to your left and the frantic, continuous call of unknown birds.

Then things begin to go off track.

First, Crush pulls a chair from the back of the Jeep, unfolds it and sits down. He takes off his hat and says: "Everyone gather round. Circle up on me." Crush takes out a large notebook and begins talking about the jungle behind you. He talks for more than half an hour. He tells a few stories about his experiences in the jungle and reads some interesting facts out of his notebook—at least, they would be interesting if you weren't standing in front of the real thing.

When Crush closes his notebook, he asks if anyone has any questions about what he just shared. No one does. Then Crush starts asking several questions of his own. He wants to know if anyone has ever been in a jungle, and what it was like. He wants to know how you react emotionally to the idea of a jungle—are you more afraid or interested? He wants you to repeat some of the facts he read out of the notebook. Sometimes he just rereads different sections when nobody seems to remember the right answer.

After a particularly long and awkward silence, Crush looks down at his watch and says: "Hey, it's getting late. We better pray and head back." Crush closes his eyes and thanks God for a safe drive out to the jungle and the chance to have a "good discussion." Then everyone piles back into the Jeep, and off you go.

Not a very satisfying safari, huh?

The reason why is obvious: your leader had a poor understanding of what he was supposed to do. He helped you get close to the jungle. He gave you some interesting information. He gave you a chance to talk with the other people in the group. But he never took you where you wanted to go—he never helped you experience anything.

That's a poor way to approach a safari, and that's a poor way to approach a small group meeting. Yet it happens every week in countless groups across the country and around the world because small group leaders have a poor understanding of their role when it comes to leading others—they think they're supposed to act mainly as teachers or hosts or facilitators or something else entirely.

If you are a small group leader, I encourage you to think of yourself as a spiritual safari guide. Your job is not to help people memorize interesting facts about God, the Bible or church history. Your job is not to get people to debate those interesting facts. Your job is not to provide a comfortable place for people to do the debating.

No, your job is to lead your group members into direct encounters with the life-changing truths written into every page of God's Word—things like faith and sin and hope and temptation and love. Your job is to help your group members grapple with those truths, understand how those truths intersect with their stories, and then make decisions and take actions based on those truths.

I've written this book to provide you with some basic principles and tools that will help you operate as a spiritual safari guide. But there's one more thing you need to keep in mind as you do so.

It's All About the Holy Spirit

As you prepare to carry out your role as a spiritual safari guide, remember this: You cannot manufacture spiritual growth within your small group members (or within yourself, actually).

No matter how good you become at leading discussion or prayer or worship or application, you cannot force your group members to grow spiritually any more than you could force them to grow taller.

The reality is that spiritual growth and transformation occur only through the supernatural work of the Holy Spirit. Jesus says a lot about this process in John 14–16, especially this passage:

> Unless I go away, the Counselor will not come to you; but if I go, I will send him to you. When he comes, he will convict the world of guilt in regard to sin and righteousness and judgment: in regard to sin, because men do not believe in me; in regard to righteousness, because I am going to the Father, where you can see me no longer; and in regard to judgment, because the prince of this world now stands condemned.
>
> I have much more to say to you, more than you can now bear. But when he, the Spirit of truth, comes, he will guide you into all truth. (John 16:7-13)

At first glance, that idea seems at odds with everything I've written up to this point. I mean, think about these two statements:

- A small group leader's primary job is to prepare for and lead small group meetings that result in spiritual growth.

- Spiritual growth can only be achieved through the work of the Holy Spirit.

Those ideas almost seem mutually exclusive, right? If small group leaders are charged with striving for a goal that only the Holy Spirit can fulfill, how can we lead well?

The answer is relatively simple: Group leaders need to lead their small group meetings in such a way that group members are able to connect with the Holy Spirit.

One of the best ways to understand this is to think about falling asleep. You can't force yourself to fall asleep. No matter how hard you try, there is no mental or physiological switch that you can flick in order to slip into unconsciousness. But you can create an environment that is conducive to sleep. You can turn the lights off, get a soft pillow, wear comfortable clothes and (if you're like me) turn on a little white noise.

Achieving transformation in your small group follows a similar dynamic. You can't force your group members to humbly seek the Holy Spirit. You can't compel the Holy Spirit to convict anyone of their sin or move into your group with a rushing wind and tongues of fire. But you can create an environment within your group meetings that is conducive to regular, life-changing encounters with the Holy Spirit—which is exactly what I mean when I talk about being a spiritual safari guide.

Again, the principles in this book will help you create that kind of environment in your group meetings, starting with chapter two—understanding the ministry of hospitality.

2

The Ministry of Hospitality

In 2002, Will Miller published a book called *Refrigerator Rights: Creating Connections and Restoring Relationships*. The book explores the loss of intimate relationships in our modern culture, citing three primary culprits: increased mobility, a heavy social emphasis on individualism, and emotionally numbing distractions (such as television and the Internet).[4]

Miller was a noted psychotherapist at Purdue University at the time of the book's publication, and it was well received in sociological circles. And because Miller was (and still is) a popular speaker and an outspoken Christian, the book also received a lot of attention from church leaders—especially those interested in the world of small groups.

Here is how Miller describes this concept of "refrigerator rights" on his blog:

> Refrigerator Rights Relationships are people who can open your refrigerator without having to ask permission. And when you are in their home you can do the same. They are people with whom you feel open, cared for, and relaxed. They know the real you behind the facade. Such relationships are critical

to a healthy life. Having "Refrigerator Rights" with someone means that you have a lifestyle that is connected and engaged. This is what too many of us are missing and yet what is necessary for a well balanced life.[5]

I need to be honest about something here: I have never been able to establish refrigerator rights with anyone outside of my family. I have actually stood in front of three different refrigerators, trying to psych myself up to take the plunge and open the door—but to no avail. All three times I shrank back and asked, "Can I grab a drink?"

Oh well. It may be that I have yet to experience the depth of relationship Miller describes. Or maybe I'm a private person and the idea of "refrigerator rights" is more of a helpful symbol than a practical benchmark.

Either way, the concept highlights an important part of your ministry as a small group leader: hospitality. That's a broad concept, one I'll be exploring more deeply in this chapter. Specifically, I'll be looking at how the following facets of hospitality will help you prepare for and lead small group meetings that result in spiritual growth:

1. the role of chores in hospitality

2. the role of prayer in hospitality

3. the necessary element of fun

One more thing: I'm writing this chapter under the assumption that the small group leaders who read it are also the primary hosts for their group meetings. That's a common practice in small groups, but I do recognize that other methods also work well. So, if your group has a separate leader and host, or if your group rotates host locations (including meeting in public spaces), then this chapter will benefit both the group leader and anyone who participates in the ministry of hospitality by hosting the group.

The Role of Chores in Hospitality

I used to think of hospitality in terms of tasks that need to be completed before a small group meeting: vacuuming the rug, washing dishes, cleaning the bathroom, baking cookies and so on. And since I don't have much affinity or affection for those tasks, I viewed hospitality as a kind of necessary evil—something that needed to be scratched off the list before I could move on to the more important work of finalizing discussion questions or preparing a prayer list.

I have repented of that decision in recent years.

One reason for this repentance is my work with SmallGroups .com, which has brought me into contact with several people who have a more mature view on the topic. I was confronted, for example, with this explanation of hospitality written by Stephanie Voiland:

> Hospitality isn't really about the physical interactions around the table with food and flatware settings (although those things certainly have their place). On a deeper level, it's more about the spiritual transactions that occur within the context of a shared home or a common meal. By this I don't necessarily mean evangelism, although that may be part of it. More than that, I want the people who cross the threshold of my home to experience a taste of Christ before they leave: a word of encouragement, a listening grace, the warmth of acceptance, an attempt at unconditional love.[6]

Another reason for my repentance is the overwhelming evidence in Scripture that hospitality is a vital ministry—one that goes way beyond vacuuming and picking my kids' toys off the floor. Think of all the significant events in the Old Testament that were preceded by an act of hospitality: Abraham and Melchizedek (Genesis 14:18-20), Rebekah and Abraham's servant (Genesis 24:12-27), Moses and Zipporah (Exodus 2:16-22), David and Abigail (1 Samuel 25:1-44), Elisha and the Shunammite woman (2 Kings 4:8-37), and there are many others. Think also of Jesus' many instructions on the subject of hospitality. Like this one from Luke 14:12-14:

> Then Jesus said to his host, "When you give a luncheon or dinner, do not invite your friends, your brothers or relatives, or your rich neighbors; if you do, they may invite you back and so you will be repaid. But when you give a banquet, invite the poor, the crippled, the lame, the blind, and you will be blessed. Although they cannot repay you, you will be repaid at the resurrection of the righteous."

Or what about this succinct promise? "I tell you the truth, anyone who gives you a cup of water in my name because you belong to Christ will certainly not lose his reward" (Mark 9:41).

And then there's this command from Jesus to his disciples, which seems to foreshadow some pretty serious consequences for people who refuse to demonstrate hospitality:

> Do not take along any gold or silver or copper in your belts; take no bag for the journey, or extra tunic, or sandals or a staff; for the worker is worth his keep.
>
> Whatever town or village you enter, search for some worthy person there and stay at his house until you leave. As you enter the home, give it your greeting. If the home is deserving, let your peace rest on it; if it is not, let your peace return to you. If anyone will not welcome you or listen to your words, shake the dust off your feet when you leave that home or town. I tell you the truth, it will be more bearable for Sodom and Gomorrah on the day of judgment than for that town. (Matthew 10:9-15)

Here's my point: hospitality is presented over and over again in the Bible as a catalyst for the movement of God and spiritual growth in the lives of his people. I think it's vital for small group leaders to understand this because I believe that spiritual growth is the primary purpose for small groups and small group meetings.

It's also vital for group leaders to understand that the root of hospitality (as presented the these Scriptures and other Bible passages) is an attitude of service and self-sacrifice. It's a willingness to offer our time, money, energy, food and even our home in an effort to love our neighbors as ourselves.

Yes, that attitude is often fleshed out through performing tasks—especially in the context of small group meetings. I want to be clear that there is nothing wrong with cleaning or vacuuming or setting the thermostat at a comfortable temperature. (Incidentally, see appendix one for a list of SmallGroups.com resources designed to make these tasks a little easier and a little more effective.)

But there is a difference between task-oriented hospitality and biblical hospitality. There is a difference between cleaning the bathroom as an act of service and cleaning the bathroom because you are embarrassed about what the other group members will think if you don't. There is a difference between baking cookies because you want to bless the people in your home and baking them because Sally used store-bought desserts last week and you think this will be more impressive.

I like how Peter approaches the subject: "Above all, love each other deeply, because love covers over a multitude of sins. Offer hospitality to one another without grumbling. Each one should use whatever gift he has received to serve others, faithfully administering God's grace in its various forms" (1 Peter 4:8-10).

So, how do you as a small group leader move away from task-oriented hospitality and toward a more biblical and robust hospitality? I'm still on that journey, but I think I have correctly identified the first step: repentance.

If you begrudge the tasks you have to perform in order to prepare for a small group meeting—the money, time and energy you spend week after week—then repent of your attitude and ask God to forgive you. Ask him to make you more like Melchizedek, Rebekah, Abigail and Jesus, so that you can offer yourself and your home as an act of love every time your group gets together.

Of course, prayer is a great way to make these requests of God. And prayer is also an important facet of hospitality.

The Role of Prayer in Hospitality

First things first: the kind of prayer I want to explore in this section is not small group prayer; it's not group members praying together during a gathering. Rather, the type of prayer that is connected to hospitality is a prayer of preparation—something the group leader (or host) does outside of a group meeting.

I'll soon offer some practical thoughts on how to carry out this method of prayer. But first I want to share some exciting research on the subject.

Survey time. Jim Egli has served for years as small group pastor of the Vineyard Church in Urbana, Illinois. But he hasn't always been confident in how to go about his role of equipping and supporting small group leaders.

Here's how Jim describes his uncertainty:

I kept hearing advice from a plethora of small-group authors and speakers, each promoting different methods and models. All of them were confident and persuasive, but their contradictory theories couldn't all be right. Someone needed to . . . cut through the confusion by doing serious, scientific research on what really creates healthy, growing small groups. We needed to look past the models to discover the key underlying principles.

I wanted to get to the bottom of things. I wanted an answer to the question, "What's the most important part of leading a small group?"[7]

So Jim did what anyone would do in that position: he completed a Ph.D. in statistical analysis, teamed up with a research partner named Dwight Marable and set out to conduct a comprehensive survey of three thousand small group leaders in over two hundred churches across the country. (Okay, so Jim is probably the only person who would do that—but I'm glad he did.)

What Jim found was both surprising and exciting, to say the least. The survey literally contained hundreds of questions that probed into every detail of a person's role as a small group leader. It covered group dynamics, leader behavior during the group meetings, leader preparation before group meetings, leader qualifications (such as having a Bible degree) and more.

And when the smoke cleared, the evidence pointed to one factor as having more influence on the spiritual health of a small group than any other: the group leader's prayer life.

Egli's survey contained hundreds of questions covering a wide range of tasks, behaviors, habits and attitudes that could be adopted or practiced by small group leaders. When he crunched the numbers, he saw right away that the following question had a high degree of correlation with a small group's spiritual health: "How much time do you spend on average praying for your small group meeting?"

Egli found several other questions that had a strong correlation with a small group's spiritual health. These five yielded the most pivotal results:

- How consistently do you take time for prayer and Bible reading?

- Are you praying daily for your non-Christian friends to come to know Jesus?

- How many days in the past week did you pray for your small group members?

- Do you pray for your group meetings in the days leading up to it?

- How much time on average do you spend in daily prayer and Bible reading?

The results led Egli to this conclusion: "The leaders whose answers revealed a strong relationship with God had groups that were healthier and faster growing. These groups experienced a deeper level of care between members, had a clearer sense of mission beyond their group, and produced more leaders and new groups."[8]

In other words, small group leaders with a strong prayer life were more likely to witness Spirit-driven growth not only in their own lives, but in the lives of their group members as well.

In addition, group leaders demonstrating strong prayer lives witnessed greater evangelistic impact within their groups. Much greater, in fact. According to the research, 83 percent of leaders with a strong prayer life reported that at least one person had come to Jesus through the influence of their group, while only 19 percent of leaders with a weak prayer life could say the same.

Of vines and branches. When I first heard about the research conducted by Egli and Marable, I was skeptical. I wondered, Could something as simple as prayer really have such a measurable impact on my small group week in and week out? But the more I thought about it, the more I realized how silly that question was.

Especially when you consider Jesus' words from John 15:4-8:

> Remain in me, and I will remain in you. No branch can bear fruit by itself; it must remain in the vine. Neither can you bear fruit unless you remain in me.
>
> I am the vine; you are the branches. If a man remains in me and I in him, he will bear much fruit; apart from me you can do nothing. If anyone does not remain in me, he is like a branch that is thrown away and withers; such branches are picked up, thrown into the fire and burned. If you remain in me and my words remain in you, ask whatever you wish, and

it will be given you. This is to my Father's glory, that you bear much fruit, showing yourselves to be my disciples.

That's the key. When you pray for the members of your small group and the event of your small group meeting, you plug into the Vine. You gain access to supernatural power. And, frankly, you get out of the Holy Spirit's way and let him do the work he wants to do.

This kind of prayer has everything to do with biblical hospitality because it involves giving your time and energy in an effort to bless others. More, through this kind of prayer you are working to "make ready" the environment of your small group meetings on a spiritual level.

I like the picture that my friend Randall Neighbor paints of these twin levels of hospitality:

> There are two other very important things you must do before your small group members arrive: work on both the physical and spiritual climate of your home. Ensure that it's cool or warm enough in your home by adjusting your thermostat. Remember that your house will be filled with people, and the collective body heat will raise the thermometer within 20 minutes of the meeting's official starting time.
>
> To adjust the spiritual temperature of your home, take five minutes to sit in the room where you will meet and ask God to fill your home with his peace, leaving no room for anything evil such as strife or discord. Invite him to come in power during the meeting. Sometimes, I will play praise music softly and pray for each member by name, asking God to touch him or her in a special way that night.[9]

Two climates: one physical, the other spiritual, and both key ingredients of biblical hospitality. Although, given the research mentioned previously, your group will be better served if you spend more of your time preparing the spiritual climate through prayer.

So let's move on to some practical thoughts on how to carry out this kind of prayer.

Preparatory prayer. People pray and connect with God in many different ways, so I'm hesitant to set any kind of limits or boundaries around how you approach this prayer of preparation. At the same time, I do understand that having a few guidelines can be helpful in getting started.

With that in mind, here are a few basic examples of how you can adjust the spiritual climate of your small group meetings through prayer:

Pray for each of your small group members every day. This is one of the most important things you can do as a small group leader. If your goal is to see group members experience spiritual growth, then the best thing you can do is intercede for them daily with the Holy Spirit.

I recommend you pray for your group members as part of your regular devotional time. Pray that they will encounter God that day. Pray for their families. Pray for their jobs. Pray for whatever challenges they have identified within the group, and praise God for whatever victories and blessings they have experienced.

I also recommend that you pray for any group members you come across throughout the course of your day. If you receive a text from someone in your group, for example, send up a quick word on their behalf: "Lord, please bless Sheila as she works today," or "Father, thank you for leading Jerry to our group."

Bracket your study times in prayer. Whenever you read over the curriculum your group is studying, start the process with prayer. Ask the Holy Spirit to give you wisdom and understanding as you explore the discussion questions or educational experiences you will be leading the group into during your next meeting. Ask that the Spirit would spur the members of the group toward obedience and application.

And when you are finished preparing for that group meeting,

pray again. Ask God to honor your efforts with spiritual fruit, to prepare the hearts of your group members and to help you be effective as you attempt to lead.

Bracket each group meeting with prayer. Before the first person walks through your door, ask the Holy Spirit to be present as your group gathers. Specifically ask the Spirit to remember the promise from Matthew 18:20: "Where two or three come together in my name, there am I with them." And after the last person leaves, pray again. Ask God to help you and your group members stay accountable when it comes to applying what you just learned.

Again, these are just a few contexts for preparatory prayer that I have found helpful in my journey as a small group leader. Be open-minded as you experiment with your own preferences and methods.

Finding the time to pray. Right about now you may be thinking, *That sounds great, but I can't spend any more time preparing for group meetings. I'm maxed out.* And I hear you. I understand that because I've been maxed out myself.

I can remember more than a few times driving to a small group meeting with my wife in the passenger seat frantically scribbling out answers in our curriculum workbook. I can also remember feeling frustrated when group members arrived early on our doorstep because I still needed to vacuum the rugs and think up an icebreaker to start the discussion.

Fortunately, I've learned some tips and tricks over the years that help me free up time for the more important elements of hospitality—like prayer. Here are some examples:

Set reasonable expectations. When it comes to preparing the physical environment of our small group meetings, I try to accomplish less than I used to. I've learned that just because there are a lot of tasks and jobs traditionally associated with leading a small group doesn't mean all of those tasks and jobs are necessary. Or that I am obligated to tackle them. Or that I am obligated to tackle them as thoroughly as others might.

For example, I don't map out the discussion portion of our group meetings as meticulously as I used to. And my wife and I have toned down the pregroup cleanup around our house. We make sure the bathroom is in good shape, of course, and we get dirty clothes and toys off the floor. But we are more willing to settle for "good enough" rather than work until everything is perfect—which means we give ourselves more time to pray.

Buy time when it's available and appropriate. If your group shares a meal together, for example, consider spending your money on a couple pizzas rather than spending an afternoon's worth of time cooking up a Thanksgiving feast. Or download a prewritten Bible study every now and then rather than writing all of your curriculum from scratch.

"Time is money" is a poor expression, but it's certainly true that money can buy some extra time for something as important as prayer.

Ask your group members for help. Many group leaders feel like they should be able to handle whatever is needed to keep the group running smoothly. Whether they want to be in control or they don't want to admit something that could be perceived as failure, they basically hog all of the ministry responsibilities within the group. But that's not healthy for the group leader or the group members. Because when participants take on additional responsibilities within the group, their level of commitment to the group rises.

So be honest with your group members. Talk to them about all of the different tasks and responsibilities you think are necessary to keep the group running smoothly. Be honest with them about the amount of time you have available and the tasks you are willing to fulfill. And then ask for help with everything that is left.

The Necessary Element of Fun

I've covered two facets of hospitality so far in this chapter:

1. Performing chores in preparation for a small group meeting can be beneficial, provided you do so out of a desire to bless others.

2. Committing to regular prayer in preparation for a small group meeting will help create a spiritual climate conducive to spiritual growth.

   Now it's time for the third facet: fun. And here's my summary statement to go along with the other two:

3. Including the element of fun in your small group meetings will help create an atmosphere that blesses others and leads to spiritual growth.

That's right! It's my belief that fun is a necessary facet of small group hospitality because it supplements and supports the other two facets.

There are two reasons why fun is crucial to a small group meeting, and everybody understands the first one. Namely, it's fun to have fun. People like having fun. You, me, your group members and anyone who might eventually become one of your group members—we all enjoy a good time.

People feel blessed when they have fun, and having fun in a small group setting creates positive associations. It helps people open up and speeds up the process of building relationships. At the very least, it gives people a concrete reason to come back even if other parts of the group meeting don't go very well. (Of course, the opposite is true for boring or overly serious group meetings.)

But there's a second reason why having fun is important for small groups, and that one is a bit more surprising. Namely, fun is a key component of spiritual growth.

Think about it: how many feasts does God command the Israelites to celebrate throughout the Old Testament? (Not "recommend," by the way, but "command.") How many parties did Jesus and his disciples attend? How many times are the members of the early church recorded as breaking bread together?

But my favorite example of this principle comes from Nehemiah 8. The Israelites had finished rebuilding the wall around Jerusalem in record time, and Nehemiah gathered them for a kind of festival of dedication. A teacher of the law named Ezra was told to read aloud from the law of Moses, and he did so "from daybreak till noon." While he read, other Levites circulated among the crowds, "making it clear and giving the meaning so that the people could understand what was being read" (Nehemiah 8:8).

What happened next was natural: the people wept. They had evidently not been exposed to the law for a long time, and they had drifted into sin yet again. So they mourned.

But not for long:

> Then Nehemiah the governor, Ezra the priest and scribe, and the Levites who were instructing the people said to them all, "This day is sacred to the LORD your God. Do not mourn or weep." For all the people had been weeping as they listened to the words of the Law.
>
> Nehemiah said, "Go and enjoy choice food and sweet drinks, and send some to those who have nothing prepared. This day is sacred to our Lord. Do not grieve, for the joy of the LORD is your strength."
>
> The Levites calmed all the people, saying, "Be still, for this is a sacred day. Do not grieve."
>
> Then all the people went away to eat and drink, to send portions of food and to celebrate with great joy, because they now understood the words that had been made known to them. (Nehemiah 8:9-12)

As a small groups guy, I love all the elements included in that account. You have people gathering together. They are exposed to the truth through God's Word. They are interacting with that truth— discussing it and learning new information. And the Spirit moves as a result, causing conviction of sin and ultimately spiritual growth.

That's a great picture of the kind of small group meeting I'm advocating in this book! And the entire event is underscored and uplifted by the element of fun.

Tips and tricks. So, what does it take to make fun a key cog in your small groups machine? Each group will have its own preferences, of course, but there are a couple of items I feel comfortable recommending. I've separated them based on the essential activities of a small group meeting I highlighted in chapter one.

Social connection and fellowship. Social connection is all about fun, of course, but a lot of times this is an unofficial portion of a group meeting—it's understood that people will "hang out" until everyone is gathered and the meeting begins.

However, I recommend making social connection an "officially sanctioned" portion of each group meeting. Make it known that you want your group members to spend time enjoying each other's company. And be sure to set a good example as the group leader by joining in the fellowship yourself.

Note that some groups like to be social at the beginning of a meeting; others like to save the fellowship until the end. But I say, Why not have both? This is just my opinion, but I think an ideal setup is to have fifteen to twenty minutes of social interaction at the beginning of the gathering. Then have an official time when the group meeting ends, but make it known that everyone is welcome to stay and hang out for as long as they'd like (or as long as is reasonable for the hosts).

Interaction with God's Word. The Bible is not a boring book, and it has a lot to say on subjects like joy and humor. Think of David's exuberant expressions throughout the Psalms, for example. Or the absurd hilarity of Jesus' story about a man with a log in his eye trying to pull a speck from the eye of someone else. Those passages are fun, and there are many others. So emphasize them in the course of your study.

Group discussion. Not all discussion questions have to be somber or deep. You can ask questions that are creative and off-the-wall—even silly. I think this is especially helpful as a way to approach Scripture passages or topics that are confusing or complex. For example: "I'll give a dollar to anyone who can name all the materials used to build the statue in Nebuchadnezzar's dream. Any takers?"

Learning activities. Learning activities provide an outlet for things like physical movement, creativity, artistic expression, competition and so on. As such, they are fertile soil for fun.

Prayer. Praise and thanksgiving are important elements of prayer, and they can both be fun—especially if you make an effort in that direction. For example, consider giving the group a chance to "shout for joy" as part of your prayer time.

Worship. Worship can be solemn and silent at times, but it can also be "a joyful noise." Or, what if you asked your group members to follow David's example of "leaping and dancing before the LORD" (2 Samuel 6:16)? How fun would that be?

Application. Sometimes it's tough to obey what you've learned about God, or it requires sacrifice. But often it's exhilarating to see God work in your life as you obey him. Plus, the reason "doing good is its own reward" is because doing good is fun—especially when you do good with a group of people you enjoy spending time with.

My point in creating this list is not to make you feel like you have to artificially inject something hilarious into every section of every group meeting. (That wouldn't be fun to plan, for one thing.) No, my point is that you don't have to compartmentalize fun into the beginning or end of your gatherings. You don't have to say, "We'll have some fun, and then we'll discuss the text, pray, sing some songs—and then we'll have fun again."

Rather, by offering a few opportunities for participants to have fun throughout your group meetings, you will bless them with a good time, and you'll take another step toward maintaining an atmosphere that is conducive to spiritual growth.

3

Learning Styles

It was just before Christmas when my son Daniel told me about a scene from one of his favorite Thomas the Tank Engine videos. "Diesel was chuffing away from Thomas," he said, "but Thomas was trying to catch him and stop him from being naughty." As he spoke, Daniel started waving his hands back and forth in front of his face, and then he clapped them together at the word *naughty*.

"Diesel went around a big curve on the mountain. He was racing very fast, and Thomas was racing very fast too." Now Daniel was rocking back and forth on his legs, and his hands were still clapping and rubbing together in front of his chest.

"Then the track was missing in front of Diesel because the bridge wasn't finished yet! Diesel tried to stop and *squeeeeeeeaaaaaaaked* with his brakes." My son pistoned his legs up and down, stretching out the word *squeaked* in a good example of onomatopoeia.

I could tell the tension in Daniel's story was rising because he literally started running around in circles as he continued to talk.

"Diesel went right to the edge, and he almost fell into the river. But he stopped. But he was hanging off the track and couldn't get back on." Daniel had finished the little circles, but now his hips were wiggling back and forth and he was chafing his fingers together like a doctor washing his hands before surgery.

"Thomas came behind Diesel and coupled up to him. Then Thomas pulled Diesel away from the hole in the tracks! Thomas was the hero and he saved Diesel!" This was the climax of the story, and Daniel sprinted away from my seat on the couch, made a circle around the dining room table, sprinted back and then collapsed next to me, breathing hard.

If someone outside of our home had seen Daniel tell his story, that person might have said my son had "ants in his pants" or had been eating too much sugar. They may have even tried to get Daniel to stand still or sit down.

But I knew that my son's wiggling and jiggling was perfectly normal. It's just one of the ways he demonstrates a strong tendency toward a kinesthetic (or physical) learning style. Meaning, whenever his brain is busy processing a lot of information (whether coming in or going out), his arms and legs want to shake and quake. For him, the process of thinking is connected to movement, which is very common for young boys.

As Daniel's father it's important that I know my son well enough to understand his learning styles so that I can use them to my advantage when I try to communicate with him—especially if I want to help him explore something important or complex. Otherwise I would be in danger of forming misconceptions about what he needs and is capable of.

Learning styles are also an important tool for leading transformational small group meetings.

A Brief Overview of Learning Styles

Here's a quick definition of learning styles to get things started:

A learning style refers to how a person perceives and processes information.

To *perceive* information refers to the way a person takes in (or receives) data from the outside world. So, we can receive data through our eyes, our ears, our nose, our fingers and so on. To *process* information refers to what a person's brain does with all of that data after it has been perceived—how the data is interpreted, categorized, stored and used.

As a small group leader, it's important that you understand how learning styles work, and how they influence your efforts at preparing for and leading small group meetings.

First, you need to understand the different types of learning styles that can be demonstrated by the members of your group. This will be vital information as you prepare to lead the essential activities for each group meeting (fellowship, interaction with God's Word, group discussion, learning activities, prayer, worship and application). Ideally, you'll get to the point where you know the specific learning styles of each person in your group, and you can tailor those essential activities to fit those preferences.

Second, you need to understand your own learning style—how you perceive and process information. This will help you get the most out of each small group meeting. It will also keep you from attempting to lead others only through the lens of your own learning style (more on that later).

The VARK Model

If you're interested in doing some research, there are several different approaches when it comes to categorizing and labeling the different learning styles. Some of these approaches are very scholarly, some are kind of silly, and a few make sense and are easy to understand. (I prefer to focus on the latter.)[10]

That's why I will be focusing on the VARK model, developed by Neil Fleming. It's a little more modern than some of the other models out there—and a little more approachable.[11]

The VARK model identifies four distinct learning styles:

- *Visual:* people who learn best through seeing
- *Aural (or Auditory):* people who learn best through hearing
- *Reading/Writing:* people who learn best through words on a page
- *Kinesthetic:* people who learn best through experience and touch

Maybe you're thinking: *Hey, I can do all of those things! I can see, hear, read, write and touch.* And that's true. But the idea behind learning styles is that you and I have preferences when it comes to the way we perceive and process information. We tend to drift more strongly toward a certain learning style—referred to as our "dominant style"—as we interact with the world. Many people also have a "secondary style" that they are comfortable learning with as well.

You can identify your dominant learning style by going to www .vark-learn.com/english/page.asp?p=questionnaire and filling out the sixteen-question assessment. (The members of your small group can do the same.)

This chapter will dig deeper into all four of the VARK learning styles, including the major characteristics of each style, how those characteristics manifest themselves in everyday life and how they can be applied to a small group setting.

But first I want to tackle the question, Why?

Why Learning Styles?

There are three important reasons why small group leaders need to have a proper understanding of learning styles:

1. *They influence how group members learn.* I know that sounds obvious—learning styles have an impact on how people learn. But it's a significant idea for both you and the other members of your group. Put simply, when your group members have a proper understanding of how they learn best, they will learn more. They will be better equipped to engage whatever curricu-

lum you are studying, and they will be better equipped to interact with and understand each other.

2. *They influence how group leaders lead.* As a small group leader,
your dominant learning style has a big influence on how you
perceive and process information from the world. But your
dominant learning style has just as much influence on how you
present that information to other people. Meaning, we tend to
teach and lead others based on the way we prefer to learn.

So, small group leaders who are dominant in the reading/
writing learning style will often structure small group meetings around activities associated with reading and writing—
making assignments in a workbook, for example, or reading
contextual information out loud. Doing so may unintentionally
ignore the needs and preferences of others in the group who
learn visually, aurally or kinesthetically. (The same is true of
group leaders with the other dominant learning styles.)

3. *They influence the interpersonal dynamics of the group.* When
people have a hard time forming a relationship because their
personalities don't mix well, we refer to it as a "personality
clash." A similar phenomenon can happen with learning
styles—especially in a small group setting where ideas are regularly explained, discussed, processed and applied. Group
members can become frustrated when others approach these
tasks in different (and sometimes competing) ways.

I'm a reading/writing learner, for example, and I can remember feeling exasperated when people in one of my earlier groups
kept rehashing the meaning of certain doctrines. I would think,
*Why don't they just read the definition written right there in the
workbook?* Looking back, I now understand those individuals
were auditory learners, and they wanted to process those definitions through conversation.

Conversely, the reality of learning styles also presents small group members with the chance to demonstrate love to each other. When we are patient with others who learn differently—and especially when we make an effort to engage others in their preferred learning styles—we are loving our group members as ourselves.

A quick side note: I made it clear in chapter one that learning information should not be the primary purpose of a small group meeting. However, I want to emphasize that the process of learning—of perceiving and processing information—is an important part of any small group meeting. That's because learning is an important part of spiritual growth, which is the primary purpose of a group meeting.

For one thing, the act of learning permeates all of the essential activities that make up an effective small group meeting. Obviously, learning plays a big part in group discussions and interactions with the Bible. But group members also learn about each other when they engage in fellowship and share pieces of their stories through prayer. And group members learn more about God when they study the Bible, work to apply what it says and worship him.

For another thing, the act of learning puts us in contact with the Holy Spirit. Here's how Jesus introduced the Spirit to the earliest leaders of the church: "The Counselor, the Holy Spirit, whom the Father will send in my name, will *teach* you all things and will remind you of everything I have said to you" (John 14:26, emphasis added).

Not only does the Spirit teach us, but as we gain new information and ideas, we give the Spirit more surface area to bring about change in our lives. As I gain understanding about the doctrines of sin and temptation, for example, I give the Holy Spirit opportunities to push me toward conviction and repentance. When I learn about the unique attributes of God, the Spirit can use that knowledge to nudge me toward greater experiences of worship and praise.

In short, under the direction of the Holy Spirit, acquiring information is an important step in the process of transformation. And that's another reason why you as a small group leader should be aware of the following learning styles.

Visual Learners

People with a visual learning style prefer to perceive information through their eyes. They like it when facts and ideas are organized visually into charts, graphs, diagrams and maps. They often communicate their thoughts through similes and metaphors that rely on images—"I was as nervous as a long-tailed cat in a room full of rocking chairs," for example.

Visual learners are also good at spatial recognition. They are aware of their physical surroundings and are able to visualize the layout of rooms and buildings. They are skilled at working with shapes and objects, even to the point of rotating and manipulating them in their mind's eye.

Visual learners often enjoy expressing themselves artistically through drawing, painting, sculpting and so forth. If they are forced to sit and listen to a lecture or take notes, you may catch them doodling shapes and patterns on their paper as a kind of "visual venting."

Here are some other cues and clues that may help you recognize a visual learner:

- If you asked a visual learner for directions, he would probably draw you a map.

- When a visual learner orders food at a restaurant, she prefers looking at the pictures on a menu, or at meals being eaten at the other tables.

- Visual learners gravitate toward books with color illustrations and complicated diagrams.

- Documents and presentations put together by a visual learner will use a wide variety of fonts, colors, images and graphs.

- A Bible owned by a visual learner may be highlighted in different colors as a method of taking notes.

- Visual learners often use these words and phrases: *vision*, *view*,

I'm trying to visualize, see the point, draw up and so on.

Visual learners in small groups. Unfortunately, much of the "traditional" small group experience does not appeal to visual learners. For one thing, few Bible studies and curriculum guides contain helpful charts, graphs or diagrams. And small group leaders often don't think to produce any kind of visual aids to supplement these materials. Many curriculum guides provide space for group members to "fill in the blank" as a method of taking notes or recording their thoughts, whereas visual learners would prefer to draw a picture or set up a chart.

In addition, most small groups are based on talking. We talk to each other during fellowship time. We discuss the Bible and what it means during study time. We verbalize our prayer requests and sing songs during worship time. While visual learners are not usually opposed to talking, they would be more stimulated and would probably retain more of what they hear if small groups included a wider variety of activities.

Here are some ways you as a small group leader can make visual learners more comfortable and more engaged:

Find visual aids. You need to make an effort to find visual aids that supplement whatever curriculum or Bible study your group is following. And if you can't find any, consider producing your own charts, graphs, diagrams—anything that puts a visual structure to facts and ideas. (Or have your visual learners produce their own chart or diagram during the group meeting.)

Use props and object lessons. Including physical objects and demonstrations in a small group meeting is another way to engage visual learners. If you are discussing how Christ is the light of the world, for example, illustrate the idea by lighting a candle in a dark room. Or set up a cross for visual learners to focus on during prayer.

Craft time. Visual learners enjoy expressing themselves artistically, so add an "arts and crafts" element to your small group every now and then. Bring in crayons and colored pencils and ask the group to draw something, or bring in Play-Doh and have them sculpt something. Of course, it won't help to have them create something random—make sure it is connected to the topic of discussion.

Use multimedia. See if you can identify a movie clip or YouTube video that would effectively illustrate the concept or idea your group will be discussing. Or have a visual group member search for one on their iPhone during the discussion.

Emphasize the visual in Scripture. Many portions of the Bible are very visual—especially the Psalms, the Prophets and apocalyptic texts like Revelation. When you notice a text that is heavy on visual elements, be sure to call them out. Make the visual nature of the verses be a large part of the discussion.

Auditory Learners

People with an auditory learning style prefer to perceive information through their ears, and they often use their mouths to process that information. They like to have concepts and ideas explained to them, and they like to explain concepts and ideas to others. That's why they are big fans of lectures (both giving and receiving). They may also be gifted at public speaking.

Auditory learners thrive in discussion-based environments. They benefit from talking through what they have learned and what they are feeling, and they are generally good at listening to others. They also enjoy participating in and listening to debates.

Many auditory learners demonstrate a strong connection to music and sounds. They often have a good sense of rhythm and enjoy singing and playing an instrument.

Here are some other cues and clues that may help you recognize an auditory learner:

• If you ask an auditory learner for directions, she will explain

in detail which roads you should take and which landmarks
to watch for.

- When an auditory learner orders food at a restaurant, he listens
  carefully when the server talks about the specials. He may also
  ask questions about different items on the menu.

- Auditory learners enjoy audio books. And if they are reading
  a hardcopy, they will probably turn on some music in the
  background.

- Cell phones are a perfect invention for auditory learners because they allow people to remain talking at almost any time
  and in almost any place.

- If an auditory learner is watching a live sports event, she may
  try to engage others around her in a conversation about what is
  happening on the field.

- Auditory learners often use these words and phrases: *I hear
  you, that sounds right, listen to me, let me explain* and so on.

Auditory learners in small groups. As you can see from the
characteristics just described, small groups are an ideal setting for
auditory learners. Whereas the traditional emphasis on talking in
small groups is a negative for visual learners, it creates a very positive atmosphere for auditory learners.

For that reason, auditory learners gravitate naturally toward
small groups, and they probably make up a large percentage of
your group.

Here's how you can make sure they benefit from the experience:

- *Discuss, discuss, discuss.* Most small groups are based on discussion, which is a big reason why small groups continue to
  grow in popularity. Continue giving your people chances to
  both talk and listen.

- *Read Scripture out loud.* For some people, reading a Bible verse
  out loud is a terrifying experience. But it is usually not the case

for auditory learners. So when your group is exploring a specific passage of Scripture, ask for volunteers to read the text out loud at least one time during the group meeting.

- *Pray out loud.* The same idea applies here. Encourage group members to pray out loud if they would like to do so.

- *Sing and make music.* I have already mentioned in an earlier chapter that small group leaders should not limit themselves to singing as an expression of worship. But that doesn't mean they should eliminate singing, either. Give your group members a chance to verbally express their devotion to God through songs, responsive readings and spontaneous prayer.

Let me say one more thing about auditory learners: don't be too quick about labeling someone in your group as a person who "talks too much." This is a common idea in small group ministry—that every group contains people who feel a need to answer every question or dominate each conversation—but it's often a misconception.

I had to grapple with this issue when Mary and her husband joined our young couples group.[12] Mary was a talker, plain and simple. Energetic and extroverted, she was the life of the party at every small group meeting, and she enthusiastically jumped into our discussions with an eagerness to learn that was refreshing to see.

She had this one habit, though. Whenever the group finished discussing a topic and started moving toward something else, she would stop everything in order to jump in and summarize what we had just talked about. Like this: "Okay, so we're saying that when Jesus talks about the kingdom of God, he's talking about our time here on earth, but also about a time in the future with the new heaven and new earth. And that's what you mean by 'already and not yet.'"

That habit annoyed me. I felt like Mary was trying to get in the last word on each issue we discussed. I felt like she was showing off. I even felt like she was usurping my role as the group leader a little bit. And because of all that, I considered confronting her about it—all in the name of improving our group experience, of course. Fortunately, I talked things through with my wife before I took any action. "She's not doing anything wrong," Jess told me. "She's just making sure she understands, and talking about it out loud probably helps her keep her thoughts straight."

We didn't know it at the time, but Jess was correctly labeling Mary as an auditory learner. Mary's habit of summing up the main ideas of our discussion was in no way malicious or self-seeking; it was a learning tool. Speaking the ideas out loud helped her process the information she heard during our discussion, just like I processed the same information by taking notes.

Not everyone is like Mary, however. There are people who legitimately "talk too much"—who dominate discussions and other activities within a small group meeting. And there are people who are socially unaware to the point that they remain ignorant when other people in the group become uncomfortable. (I'll give some guidance on helping these people in chapter ten.)

But before you label someone as "too talkative"—and definitely before you approach that person in an effort to have him or her talk less—take a step back and make sure you are evaluating the situation correctly. Is that person's behavior really causing damage to your small group? Or is he or she simply operating normally in their preferred style of learning?

Reading/Writing Learners

People with a reading/writing learning style choose to perceive and process information by—well, reading and writing. If they were assigned to learn something, they would go straight to a book and research the given topic. If they were asked to explain a concept or idea to another person, they would summarize what they have read about that concept or idea. And when they listen to a lecture or sermon, they process that auditory experience by writing down copious notes.

Reading/writing learners even turn to books as a means of artistic enjoyment and expression. They enjoy literature and good prose, and they often collect vast libraries (when they can afford it). They can write both creatively and practically, moving from a grocery list to poetry without any need to change gears.

Here are some other cues and clues that may help you recognize a reading/writing learner:

- If you ask a reading/writing learner for directions, he will jot down the appropriate streets and turns in list form.

- When a reading/writing learner orders food at a restaurant, she reads the menu and decides what she wants.

- Reading/writing learners place a high value on well-written quotations and clever word games.

- Reading/writing learners also place a high value on published authors, often desiring to write their own books one day.

- People who spend a lot of time making to-do lists are often reading/writing learners.

- A reading/writing learner would rather e-mail you or text message you than call your cell phone.

Reading/writing learners in small groups. As with auditory learners, small groups present a lot of advantages to people with a reading/writing learning style.

The idea of a Bible study or curriculum guide is exciting for reading/writing learners, as is the opportunity to study the Bible directly. These individuals also enjoy the traditional "inductive Bible study" format, where they are asked to read a portion of the text, interpret what it means and then make a connection toward application.

Reading/writing learners usually enjoy small group discussions—especially when they are given the opportunity to recite definitions, make connections to other parts of Scripture and dig into the study notes contained in their Bibles.

Here are some more ways to maximize a small group experience for reading/writing learners:

- *Homework.* I know, I know. For a lot of people, *homework* is a dirty word. But not for reading/writing learners. They don't like making spontaneous judgments about a text and would prefer to study, take notes and answer questions during the week in order to be fully prepared for the group discussion.

  So don't totally abandon the idea of homework—but don't make it mandatory for all of your group members, either. Make it an option.

- *Reading time.* If your small group is approaching a Bible passage or a book for the first time, be sure to provide a few minutes for people to read it over more than once. Give your reading/writing learners the time they need to dig in.

- *Write on the board.* You may want to consider including a whiteboard or tear-off notepad in your small group sessions. Ask someone to take notes during the discussion so that the primary ideas and opinions being shared are written out for everyone to see.

- *Give tests and evaluations.* Again, this will probably not be a popular feature of your group if you do it every week. But there is value in writing up a little quiz before your group begins a new curriculum series in order to see what your group members already know. And there is value in another quiz or evaluation after the series is over in order to see what they have retained. (Your reading/writing learners will also like it if you set up a game based on *Jeopardy* or *Trivial Pursuit.*)

Kinesthetic Learners

People with a kinesthetic learning style (also called a tactile learning style) prefer to process information through their fingers and skin. They are hands-on and would choose to participate in physical activities rather than listen to a lecture or participate in a debate. They learn well when they can manipulate physical objects and conduct experiments.

Kinesthetic learners usually don't like trying to explore abstract theories or ideas. They prefer to be more concrete and practical. "Practice makes perfect" would be an ideal motto for a kinesthetic learner.

Kinesthetic learners also place a high value on experience. They hold things to be more true when they have experienced them, and they would prefer others to tell stories about their experiences rather than give opinions on matters in which they are not experts.

Here are some other cues and clues that may help you recognize a kinesthetic learner:

- If you ask a kinesthetic learner for directions, she just may offer to take you to the destination herself.

- When a kinesthetic learner orders food at a restaurant, he prefers to choose something he has eaten at that restaurant before—something he has already experienced.

- A kinesthetic learner would rather hold a book in her hand than read something from a screen. She may also trace her finger along the page as she reads, and she enjoys the act of folding and refolding a newspaper.

- Kinesthetic learners enjoy sports and other activities that allow them to engage their bodies with the world around them. Gardening would be a good example.

- A kinesthetic employee would prefer to watch his boss demonstrate what needs to be done rather than read a manual or listen to his boss explain the task.

- If you've heard a story of a child taking apart a telephone or alarm clock and then trying to put it back together, he or she was probably a kinesthetic learner.

- Kinesthetic learners use these words and phrases: *application, get my hands dirty, that feels right, it's been my experience that* and so on.

Kinesthetic learners in small groups. There are many aspects of participating in a small group that are unappealing to kinesthetic learners. First and foremost would be staying seated in the same place for a long period of time. The traditional method of "going around the circle" for prayer requests is also disagreeable for kinesthetic learners because it takes so long for everyone to talk about what's on their mind, and then everyone to pray out loud.

Kinesthetic learners can also become frustrated when a small group spends most of its time talking and discussing and debating. They want to move quickly into application. They want to get out of the living room and do something.

Here are some ways that you can improve the experience of kinesthetic learners in your small group:

- *Service projects.* Kinesthetic learners are great for small groups because they are often the ones pushing others to "practice what they preach." They want to get out into the world and make an impact based on what the group has been learning.

- *Establish mentoring relationships.* Paul's admonition to "follow my example, as I follow the example of Christ" (1 Corinthians 11:1) sounds just right to kinesthetic learners. Rather than establish some kind of amorphous accountability within the whole small group, kinesthetic learners do well when they can be in a "do as I do" relationship with another disciple of Jesus—both as the mentor and the mentee.

- *Move around.* Sitting still is not a preferred activity for kinesthetic learners, so build in some activities that provide people a chance to move their bodies. Announce a stretch break for five minutes before the discussion starts. Encourage people to get down on their knees or walk around during the prayer time.

- *Give them something to hold.* A kinesthetic learner will do much better during a "sit and talk" activity if they have something in their hands to hold, squeeze, bend or throw. So consider making one or more of these materials available at each small group meeting: a small ball, pipe cleaners, Play-Doh, a Rubik's Cube—anything that can be physically manipulated while a person sits and participates in a discussion.

Multimodal Learners

In addition to a dominant learning preference, most people feel comfortable perceiving and processing information through at least one other learning style—what is called a "secondary" learning style. Neil Fleming refers to these individuals as multimodal learners, and his research indicates that more than half of people who take the VARK questionnaire demonstrate at least one secondary learning style.[13]

Many multimodal learners act is if they have two, three or even four dominant learning styles. Meaning, they can switch back and forth between their preferences in order to best match the information that needs to be learned.

I am a reading/writing learner, for example, but I also have a secondary kinesthetic learning preference. When my lawnmower breaks, which seems to happen every summer, I am comfortable with trying to diagnose the problem by taking the engine apart and looking for something out of place—this is a kinesthetic approach. I find this more efficient than reading about potential problems and then taking the engine apart, which would be the reading/writing approach.

Some multimodal learners aren't able to switch back and forth between learning styles, but rather attempt to gather and process information using several styles at once. These individuals often learn at a slower pace, because they have to synthesize different types of information gleaned from different types of sources. When they complete the process, however, they often have a tighter grip on what they've learned than others who operate in one style at a time.

All in all, the presence of multimodal learners is good news for small group leaders. That's because group members with a multi-modal preference are able to learn in more than one way, which means they feel more comfortable in a greater number of activities during a small group meeting.

Social and Solitary Learners

In addition to the four learning styles included in the VARK model, people also prefer learning in either a social or solitary environment.

There's not a lot to explain with these terms. Social learners prefer to be around other people. They learn best when they can talk with others or participate in activities with other people. They seem to gain energy when they are in a crowd of people and are less motivated to learn when they are alone.

Solitary learners are just the opposite. Given a preference, they would prefer to perceive and process information by themselves, and they retain that information best when they don't have a lot of distractions around them. Solitary learners can "burn the mid-night oil" reading by themselves or taking apart a complicated machine, but they become drained when they are expected to be part of a crowd for more than a short amount of time.

Obviously, a small group setting is better suited for social learners. And that probably means that a large percentage of people in your small group are social learners. If you give them opportunities to connect, talk and experience the group together, they will be happy.

Most solitary learners will not have a problem being part of a small group for one or two hours each week—they aren't hermits who never want to be exposed to other human beings. But it is true that social environments are not the ideal place for them to learn new ideas and concepts, or to accurately process different experiences.

So here are a couple things you can do to assist the solitary learners in your small group:

- *Homework.* Again, some people really do prefer to study and engage a book or curriculum guide during the week. For solitary learners the chance to get acquainted with the discussion material by themselves will limit the amount of distraction they feel when participating with the whole group.

- *Subgroup.* It's often a good idea to split your small group into smaller subgroups, with each subgroup containing between two and four people. This provides a more intimate experience for prayer, worship or discussion. And for solitary learners, it minimizes potential distractions and doesn't drain their energy as quickly as a larger group would.

- *Minimize the pressure.* Small groups in general are viewed as a social experience, which means people are expected to "pitch in" and "get involved." For that reason, many group leaders become nervous when one or two people don't say very much in a group, or when those people leave right after the group ends instead of staying to chat. But those behaviors would be natural for a person with a preference toward solitary learning. So don't apply a lot of pressure aimed at getting everyone to participate on an equal basis. Let solitary learners ease in at their own pace.

Engaging Multiple Learning Styles in a Small Group

If you have a mind for math, I can guess what you are probably thinking right now. *Let's see: four dominant learning styles, plus multimodal learners, plus a choice between solitary or social learning. That's dozens of possible combinations when it comes to the learning preferences in my small group! How in the world can I plan for all those?*

Believe me, the last thing I want to do is make life more difficult or more time-consuming for small group leaders. That is not the goal of this chapter; that is not the goal of this book.

That's why I am happy to say that it only takes two steps to prepare for each group meeting in a way that engages all the varied learning styles of your group members.

Step one: Check for gaps. The first thing to do is review your Bible study plan or curriculum guide and identify which learning styles will be targeted throughout the session. For example, if you're using a Bible study that opens with an icebreaker activity where people get up and walk around, you know that activity will appeal to kinesthetic learners. Then, if the study contains several questions later on that will help you facilitate a discussion, you know that will appeal to auditory learners.

You'll want to make a mental note of these connections at the very least. But I recommend you take it a step further and write a *K* next to the icebreaker and an *A* next to the discussion questions. That way you have a quick reminder that the kinesthetic and auditory learning styles have been targeted.

Note that it's possible for one segment of the curriculum guide to appeal to multiple learning styles at the same time. Meaning, an icebreaker where all of your group members walk around and talk to each other about their childhood memories would connect with kinesthetic, auditory and social learners. So you would write *K*, *A* and *Social* next to that icebreaker.

When you finish reviewing the study, just look back and see how many times each learning style has been targeted. And, more importantly, check to see which learning styles have not been targeted.

If you don't see any *V*'s, for example, you know there is a gap in that Bible study for visual learners. If there are ten *A*'s, that means the study is overbalanced toward auditory learners.

Step two: Find a balance. Once you've identified the gaps in a given Bible study or curriculum guide, take a few moments to plan some additional elements or activities that fill in those gaps.

For example, I mentioned before that a lot of prewritten curriculum guides do a poor job of appealing to visual learners. If that's the case with your particular study, find a YouTube clip that connects with the topic of discussion. Or find household objects that can provide a visual association to doctrines or concepts—a pair of scissors to show the need to cut sin out of our lives, a loaf of bread to remind us that the Bible is part of our spiritual nourishment, and so on.

In a similar way, pay attention if your study guide has an imbalance toward one or more learning styles. For example, I mentioned that marking down ten *A*'s shows that a study is pretty heavily favored toward auditory learners. In that situation, just cross out a few of the elements that don't seem necessary. Plan on skipping them in favor of a more balanced approach.

One of the best ways to maintain a balanced approach to your preparation for each group meeting is to emphasize the use of icebreakers and learning activities. That's because they often appeal to multiple learning styles, as was the case with the childhood memories example. The key is to connect these icebreakers and activities with the central topic of the group's discussion—something I discuss in detail throughout chapter five.

Another way to maintain a balanced approach in your lesson

preparation is to add layers to the existing elements already contained in your Bible study. Instead of thinking up a whole new activity that would appeal to kinesthetic learners, just add a layer of physical movement to something that is already part of your plan. Have people toss a ball back and forth during the discussion time, for example. Whoever is holding the ball has the floor to speak, and he or she can toss the ball to the next person with something to say.

Finally, if you feel like the study is fairly balanced without you doing any extra work—that's great. You're golden. Don't spend any more time on this than you have to.

An Important Public Service Announcement

I don't want to end this chapter without making one thing very clear: *Small group leaders should not try to make every part of a group meeting appeal to all possible learning styles.* That is not a realistic goal, and it's not something that would be very helpful even if you were able to achieve it.

As I mentioned before, every person in your small group has the capacity to perceive and process information through all four of the VARK learning styles. Yes, each group member has a dominant learning style that he or she prefers to operate in. Yes, it is likely that group members will become bored, uncomfortable or disconnected if they sit through an entire group meeting without any connection to that dominant learning style.

But that's all they really need: a connection. A taste. A chance to operate in their element here and there.

So concentrate on leading your group through gatherings that are balanced as a whole. Give your group members one or two experiences each meeting that allow them to think and learn in the ways that are most natural to them. Doing so will go a long way toward creating an environment where the Holy Spirit can operate, and where each person can grow.

PART TWO

Planning Your Route

I have led more than five hundred small group meetings over the past ten years, and I can honestly say that I have engaged in some form of preparation for every one of them.

Sometimes that preparation has been thorough, involving commentaries and concordances and hours of extra work. Other times that preparation has been hurried and harassed—scribbling down notes and Scripture references on scratch sheets of paper while the first group member pulls into the driveway. Mostly it has been somewhere in the middle.

In many ways, each act of preparing for a group meeting has been an experience unique unto itself. Each one involved a different combination of material to be explored, including Scripture passages and other books, plus a different collection of group members to join me in the exploring.

But I've also developed a general routine that I follow as I prepare for group gatherings week in and week out. This routine includes a handful of activities that help me map out a plan for each group meeting—a strategy that lets me determine ahead of time where I hope to go and what I hope to accomplish.

The five chapters in part two of this book are designed to give you an overview of those activities so that you can develop your own plan for each small group meeting:

- Chapter four introduces the "big idea" as an important part of preparing for (and leading) a group meeting.

- Chapter five offers advice on using icebreakers and learning activities.

- Chapter six explains how to write discussion questions that actually spark discussion.

- Chapter seven examines what is required when preparing for times of worship and prayer within your group meetings.

- Chapter eight helps you put everything together in a final plan and explains the danger of unintended curriculum.

4

The Big Idea

Take a moment to consider another scenario involving Crush, our fictional safari guide:

> Crush gathers your group together and, thankfully, leads you into the jungle this time. You begin walking down a narrow path, and Crush explains some interesting facts about different plant species you find along the way.
>
> After a few minutes, one of the people in your group asks Crush if there are any monkeys in this part of the jungle, and he answers yes. He even offers to lead everyone to a tribe of howler monkeys living nearby. Along the way, however, another group member spots a brightly colored lizard, which Crush unsuccessfully attempts to catch for several minutes.
>
> The chase has led your group off the path, but Crush knows a shortcut to the howler monkeys, and he strikes off with everyone in tow. Suddenly a parrot lands on a nearby branch, and Crush launches into an extended explanation on the details of its plumage and diet. This does not sit well with the group member who wanted to see the monkeys, and he begins to scowl and loudly clear his throat in protest.

When the bird finally flies away, Crush leads the group on a long hike until you are within sight of the howler monkeys' main tree. Unfortunately, Crush remembers too late that howlers are nocturnal, and so all you can see are a few fuzzy lumps sleeping peacefully among the branches.

There is no time left to strike off in search of other interesting creatures, and so Crush leads you and the rest of the group back to your camp.

How would you feel about that safari experience? It could have been worse, certainly. You were able to go into the jungle this time. And yet the entire event suffered from a lack of direction, which resulted in a lot of wandering coupled with a few moments of interesting activity.

The same thing can happen in your small group meetings if you do not commit to preparing a useable plan ahead of time. And your first step in preparing that plan should be to identify a "big idea."

Defining Terms

The concept of a "big idea" is not difficult or complicated:

The "big idea" is the main premise you want to explore with your small group during a given meeting.

Here's another way to say it: the "big idea" is the main principle you would want participants to remember from a group meeting if you knew they would forget everything else.

For example, imagine how the preceding safari scenario would have been different if Crush had determined ahead of time that his main goal was to help the group experience the tribe of howler monkeys. He could have incorporated information about the lizard and the parrot during the group's journey without allowing them to become a distraction. He also could have approached the monkeys in a way that allowed the group to experience them best. (Namely, closer to nightfall.)

In the same way, you will have the most success as a leader if you identify a specific idea or theme you want your group members to encounter during their time together. That theme can be as simple as, We're going to explore the doctrine of grace, for example. Or even, We're going to read Romans 3 and see how it applies to our lives. Your "big idea" can be topical, especially if your group is studying a book. Something like, We're going to talk about forgiveness in marriage.

The point is this: One of your main tasks as a small group leader is to help your group members stay focused as they explore that idea or theme—it's your job to prevent the group from wandering around aimlessly. And having a "big idea" allows you to do that job well.

I want to make one more thing clear before I go any further: working with a "big idea" should not be overly complicated or time consuming. It should not be a burden or an obstacle you have to overcome during the process of preparing for a small group meeting.

Rather, a "big idea" is a simple decision that helps you stay focused as you prepare for and lead a small group meeting. It's the difference between saying, "We're going to eat dinner at Joe's Crab Shack," and "We're going to drive around downtown and see if we can find a place to eat."

The Educational Benefits of a Big Idea

Beyond sharpening your focus, having a "big idea" will also provide an educational benefit for your small group meetings. That's because everyone attending those meetings (including you) will be a human being. And human beings are controlled by human brains. And most human brains have a hard time processing and retaining a large amount of information in a small amount of time.

Here's a quick experiment to show you what I mean: think back to the last time you attended a worship service at your church. (I'm talking about the Sunday-morning experience with the senior pastor and a parking lot, not a small group meeting.) See if you can answer these questions in connection with that service:

1. What did you eat for breakfast that morning?

2. Can you name three people you talked to before, during or after that service (not including your family)?

3. How many songs did the worship team lead?

4. What was the main Scripture reference in your pastor's sermon?

5. How many of your pastor's bullet points can you remember?

If you're feeling good, keep moving back in time. Can you answer those questions about the sermon you attended two weeks ago? A month ago? I can't either.

The same experiment can work with the last small group meeting you were a part of:

1. Who was the first person to arrive at the meeting?

2. Can you name three prayer requests made by group members other than you (or your family)?

3. Which concepts interested you the most during the discussion?

4. Can you answer the same questions about a group meeting you participated in more than a month ago?

Here's the reality: people forget the majority of what they hear from their pastor during each week's sermon. And they forget the majority of what they hear and discuss during your small group meetings. This happens because those events are usually packed with more information than you or I can reasonably process and retain over time.

I remember one gathering where the group spent fifteen minutes talking about justification. I had prepared a definition beforehand, and several people worked through the doctrine in their own words—how it applied to salvation, how it was different from sanctification and so on. The very next week I was introducing the idea that Abraham was justified by faith (Romans 4) when someone asked, "What does *justified* mean?"

That was frustrating. I had put a lot of effort into planning those group meetings, after all—a lot of time and energy. And it was deflating to learn that my group members were not retaining much of what we discussed. It made me feel like giving up. Maybe you're feeling the same way right now.

But giving up and canceling your small group is not a good solution to this problem. Neither is trying to "dumb things down" so that your group members won't forget the majority of what is discussed. No, the answer is to help your group members understand, retain and apply the elements of each group meeting that are most important.

What you can do is structure each group meeting so that your people are confronted with one vital principle over and over, which gives them more opportunities to engage and interact with that principle. It also provides more opportunities for the Holy Spirit to make an impact in your group and help everyone, you included, retain that principle and apply it to your lives in a way that produces spiritual growth.

And that is why you need a "big idea."

How to Identify the "Big Idea"

Identifying a "big idea" for a particular group meeting really involves just two steps:

1. Read through (or watch) the material to be covered in that meeting.

2. Pick a direction from within that material that best fits the needs and current trajectory of your group.

If you are writing a Bible study from scratch, then the material you need to read through is just the Scripture passage(s) for the group meeting, plus whatever supplemental resources you plan on using—books, commentaries, websites and so on (more on that soon). If you are using a book or prewritten curriculum, then you'll need to read through that as well.

One of the nice things about prewritten curriculum is that the authors usually do a lot of spadework for you in terms of approaching the group meeting in an organized way. In my review of study guides in recent years, I've found more and more studies that provide a central theme or idea for each group session—usually you find it in the introductory material or even with the title. If that's the case, chances are good that this theme will serve as your "big idea" (although you may want to tweak it to match the specific needs of your group).

Even if your curriculum doesn't have a central theme, most study guides provide between two and five main points for each session, with discussion questions and activities divided between those points. That gives you a solid roadmap of the concepts that will be up for discussion, and you can create your own "big idea" by finding the common element between those main points—or by focusing on one or two main points and eliminating the rest.

A Quick Word About Research

Part of the process of identifying a "big idea" is becoming familiar enough with the material to make educated decisions about what you want to happen during a group meeting. And that usually means doing a bit of research—especially if you are writing your own curriculum.

Commentaries, sermons, footnotes and everything in between are useful in sparking ideas and helping you focus your thoughts. But the question I often hear from small group leaders is: How much research is enough?

There's no easy way to answer that question. Some group leaders go crazy, reading supplementary materials for hours in preparation for a group meeting. Others don't read anything except the Bible verses that will be under discussion. My general opinion is that the best approach lies somewhere in the middle.

I like to have Bible study tools available to answer questions that occur to me as I read the text. And I do read commentaries to get a sense of what the experts think about any Scripture passages that will be featured in a group meeting—but I almost always read commentaries last so that I can gather my own thoughts instead of defaulting to whatever the experts say. All together, I rarely spend more than twenty to thirty minutes reading "outside" material in preparation for a small group meeting.

Really, the point of adding research to your preparation for a group meeting is to help you feel more confident in your understanding of the material that will be explored. You want to make sure you're not turning your back on basic doctrines or reading more into a text than is actually there. You also want to gain some information about the context of your Scripture passages so that you can pass some of that along to your group members and have a shot at answering some of the questions they ask.

One more thing about research before a small group meeting: make an effort to find quality sources. Google and Wikipedia are wonderful tools, but there is a lot of questionable material available on the Internet—a lot of bad theology and lazy opinions that can knock both you and your group off track. Published books don't always contain helpful or accurate information, but at least they have gone through a process of peer review.

The best thing to do is find an author or series of resources that you connect with and trust—especially ones that have been recommended and approved by other scholars and theologians.

Case Study

I recently led a group through a study on the book of James. Throughout part two of this book, I will spend a portion of each chapter re-creating the steps I took to prepare for the group meeting that focused on James 3:1-12. (Think of it as an extended case study.) In order to maintain consistency, all examples will refer to the same portion of Scripture, and I will carry the progress from each chapter over to the next.

My first step in preparing for that group meeting was to read through the source material and identify a "big idea." So, here is the text:

> Not many of you should presume to be teachers, my brothers, because you know that we who teach will be judged more strictly. We all stumble in many ways. If anyone is never at fault in what he says, he is a perfect man, able to keep his whole body in check.
>
> When we put bits into the mouths of horses to make them obey us, we can turn the whole animal. Or take ships as an example. Although they are so large and are driven by strong winds, they are steered by a very small rudder wherever the pilot wants to go. Likewise the tongue is a small part of the body, but it makes great boasts. Consider what a great forest is set on fire by a small spark. The tongue also is a fire, a world of evil among the parts of the body. It corrupts the whole person, sets the whole course of his life on fire, and is itself set on fire by hell.
>
> All kinds of animals, birds, reptiles and creatures of the sea are being tamed and have been tamed by man, but no man can tame the tongue. It is a restless evil, full of deadly poison.

With the tongue we praise our Lord and Father, and with it we curse men, who have been made in God's likeness. Out of the same mouth come praise and cursing. My brothers, this should not be. Can both fresh water and salt water flow from the same spring? My brothers, can a fig tree bear olives, or a grapevine bear figs? Neither can a salt spring produce fresh water.

As I read through the passage several times, I began filtering out some of the major concepts and ideas it addresses:

- responsibility for teachers
- control
- the tongue
- speaking and using words
- good and evil
- danger/poison
- praising and cursing
- hypocrisy

Any of these themes would have made an interesting and potentially helpful "big idea," especially if I wanted the group to concentrate on a smaller section of Scripture. For example, I could have focused on verses 1-2 and condensed the meeting to an exploration on the role and responsibility of teachers. Instead, I chose to delve into all twelve verses, which required a broader "big idea."

Here is what I eventually came up with: *the words we speak can accomplish powerful things both for good and evil.* That was the main idea I wanted to explore with the members of my group during that particular meeting. If we didn't accomplish anything else, I wanted us to at least grapple with that truth.

Incidentally, it's common to find several good options for a potential "big idea" as you begin to explore the material for a group meeting—especially if you are looking at a book or passage of Scripture that is as diverse as James 3. In those situations, you have to make a choice based on what will be most applicable and helpful for your group.

If my group had spent several weeks studying the doctrine of sin, for instance, I may have chosen to focus the meeting on why the tongue is "a world of evil among the parts of the body."

In the end, identifying a "big idea" will provide considerable dividends throughout your preparations for a small group meeting—as you'll see in the remaining chapters of this section.

5

Icebreakers and Learning Activities

I was skimming through the book of Revelation in preparation for another small group meeting when I came across this verse: "Wake up! Strengthen what remains and is about to die, for I have not found your deeds complete in the sight of my God" (Revelation 3:2).

I really liked the impact of those first two words: "Wake up!" And they gave me an idea for a good way to start the discussion on that chapter. So, at the beginning of our next group meeting, I told everyone I had a challenge to announce: "I will give five dollars to any person who can fall asleep in the next five minutes," I said. "Any takers?"

There were two volunteers. One of them laid on the floor and the other tried to snuggle into his corner of the couch. While they attempted to lose consciousness, I asked the other members of the group to talk about the rituals they went through each night to prepare for bed.

When five minutes had passed, I said, "I would like everyone who is awake to please raise their hand." Both volunteers sat up and put their hands in the air—accompanied by a few good-natured jeers from the other group members, of course. (Not from me, though. I was just thankful to be keeping my money.)

After everything calmed down a bit, I asked, "What happened? Can either of you explain why you weren't able to fall asleep?" Both of them had similar answers—they were distracted by the conversation from the rest of the group, and their minds were overly active because they couldn't stop thinking about falling asleep. One of them actually said, "It's easy to wake up on command, but not the other way around."

That was my cue to say, "Well, thanks to both of you for trying. Now let's all open our Bibles to Revelation 3, and we'll take a look at an entire church that was commanded to wake up."

In my opinion, that story demonstrates an effective use of a learning activity (in this case an icebreaker) to supplement the discussion portion of a small group meeting. I'll use the rest of this chapter to explain why I think so—and to offer some tips and techniques that will help you plan similar activities for your own group.

Defining Terms

The first thing I want to make clear is that I view *learning activity* and *icebreaker* as similar terms, but slightly different.

Learning activity is the broader term, and it encompasses any educational activity within a small group meeting that goes beyond discussion. So, learning activities have two key characteristics:

- They are educational, which means they are intended to help you and the other members of your group interact with truths and ideas that can be learned.

- They go beyond discussion, which means they involve more than talking or debating about those truths and ideas. Learning activities incorporate additional attributes, such as physical movement, artistic expression, humor, competition and so on.

That means there are all kinds of activities that can be considered learning activities within a small group meeting. Examples include games, role play, object lessons, drawing, music, making crafts and more. Even something as crazy as trying to get group members to fall asleep can work well as a learning activity within the boundaries of a small group.

This diversity makes learning activities an invaluable element of small group meetings because they help people with different learning styles engage in the topics being explored by the group. As I mentioned in chapter three, people with an auditory learning style would generally be happy to spend one or two hours talking about important issues and ideas. But visual, reading/writing and kinesthetic learners need to go beyond discussion in order to feel comfortable and engaged. Learning activities help them do that.

In addition, most learning activities provide an opportunity for fun. They let group members interact with each other in diverse and creative ways—ways that go beyond sitting and talking—which is usually enjoyable.

In terms of frequency, I almost always plan at least one learning activity for each group meeting I lead (usually an icebreaker), but I seldom plan more than two.

Exploring Icebreakers

An *icebreaker* is a specific type of learning activity—one that occurs at the beginning of a small group meeting, or at the beginning of the discussion portion of a small group meeting. Icebreakers serve an introductory role. Meaning, they move people toward the truths and ideas that will be explored in a group meeting (whereas a general learning activity could be a way of interacting with an idea or truth after it has already been introduced).

I want to zero in on icebreakers for a moment because I place a high value on their use within small groups. In fact, I incorporate an icebreaker into the beginning of every small group meeting I lead (and have done so for years).

Beyond appealing to multiple learning styles and allowing for fun, icebreakers offer three unique benefits to small group leaders.

Icebreakers provide a transition from the outside world. It would be great if every person walked into a small group meeting ready to be a small group member—fully engaged with the study material and eager to participate. But that doesn't always happen. Maybe Steve walks in feeling stressed because he had a rough day at the office. Or Mary and James have a six-month-old who doesn't sleep through the night, which means they both feel exhausted. Or Sheila is still thinking about the end of a fascinating movie she just saw.

In reality, everybody who attends your small group meeting brings with them the potential for serious distraction. Including you. But an icebreaker helps people transition away from those distractions and into the life of the group. It allows people to focus on something creative or humorous or physical, which begins taking their attention away from whatever was happening "outside."

They become a trigger for engagement in the group meeting. Do you remember Pavlov's famous experiment with dogs? Ivan Pavlov was a physiologist who used a variety of stimuli (including ringing a bell) whenever he brought food to a select group of dogs. Pretty soon the dogs began to salivate whenever he rang that bell, regardless of whether he had food or not. The ringing bell triggered a specific response.

A similar thing can happen with icebreakers (although it shouldn't involve drooling). When you consistently begin your group meetings with an icebreaker, your group members will quickly normalize that experience. They will expect it; they will anticipate it. More importantly, they will connect the icebreaker to the other elements of your group time. Just like Pavlov's dogs connected the ringing bell with eating, your group members will connect the experience of an icebreaker with relational connection, discussion, worship, prayer, application and so on.

This means the icebreaker will trigger your group members to prepare for engagement in those activities. Without thinking about it, they will open up relationally. Their minds will begin to focus in preparation for discussion. They will begin to think about God in preparation for prayer and worship. In other words, they will get ready to fully engage in the different activities of the group meeting.

They encourage people to arrive on time. Many group leaders start their meetings with anywhere from ten to thirty minutes of fellowship time. This can be a good practice, but it can also train people to arrive late. If your group is supposed to start at 7 p.m., for example, you will have some members begin arriving at 7:10 or 7:15. They'll think, *It's not a big deal; I'm just missing a little bit of fellowship time.*

But pretty soon they will plan on arriving at 7:15, and then one day something will happen that makes them arrive later than they planned, and they'll enter the meeting at 7:30. When this starts happening to several of your group members, punctuality becomes a big problem.

Using an icebreaker at a specific time every gathering—at 7:30, for example—is a great way to contend with this problem. Doing so provides group members with both a positive incentive for arriving on time (icebreakers are interesting and fun) and a negative incentive for arriving late (missing the icebreaker means missing the introduction to the meeting's theme).

A Problem with Icebreakers

Because of my experiences in the world of small groups, I've had the opportunity to read and evaluate a large number of the Bible studies and curriculum guides available for small group leaders to purchase. And while many of these resources contain useful material, very few of them offer group leaders any help when it comes to the kinds of learning activities described in this chapter.

True, many Bible studies do provide an icebreaker at the beginning of each session. But most of these consist of a single question designed to be answered by each person in the group. "What was your favorite color as a child?" for example. Or "If you could go on vacation anywhere in the world, where would you go?"

Sometimes the question may involve multiple choices:

If God made you an animal instead of a human being, what would you be?

- a lion

- a mouse

- a sloth

- a whale

- a bee

To be fair, these kinds of questions can provide some valuable insights at the beginning of a group's journey together. They can help people get to know each other through the sharing of stories, dreams and fears.

But it's been my experience that these icebreaker questions quickly become stale. I remember using the "What was your favorite color as a child" question with one of my earlier small groups, for example. The participants went around the circle giving one-word answers with the efficiency of a machine gun: "Red." "Green." "Yellow." "Yellow." "Pink." "Green." "Purple." "Blue."

I struggled for thirty seconds or so to think of a follow-up question, and for a moment I was on the verge of asking, "Well, what's your favorite color now?" Mercifully, however, I thought better of it and dove into the discussion questions instead.

Sadly, as barren as published curriculum can be in terms of robust and helpful icebreakers, the landscape is positively desolate when it comes to providing additional learning activities within a study. Indeed, excluding what is available on Small

Groups.com, I can count on two hands the number of curriculum guides I've seen that included any kind of learning activity in the middle or at the end of a session.

Here's what that means: if you want to include full-bodied icebreakers or learning activities within your small group meetings, you will probably have to come up with those activities yourself. And that's true even if you purchase a published Bible study.

Don't be afraid, though. Writing effective icebreakers and learning activities is much easier than it may seem at first—especially after you practice a few times and start getting the hang of it.

To that end, I'll spend the rest of this chapter highlighting what I have found to be the key steps in the process of creating helpful learning activities, along with a few techniques that have served me well week in and week out. To aid this process, I will continue the case study from James 3 that I began in chapter four.

Step One: Identify Core Concepts

I mentioned earlier that one of the main benefits of using learning activities within a group meeting is that they help you and your group members explore key concepts more deeply. Therefore, the first step in writing an effective learning activity is to identify the key concepts you would like to explore in a given meeting.

Returning to the analogy of small group leaders as spiritual safari guides, this act of identifying core concepts would be like choosing the specific animals you plan on visiting during an excursion into the jungle. You are making a rough map of the different truths and ideas you hope to interact with during a group meeting.

The good news is that you may have already completed this step while identifying a big idea. For example, in the case study I started in chapter four, I identified the following major concepts while exploring James 3:1-12:

- responsibility for teachers
- control
- the tongue
- speaking and using words
- good and evil
- danger/poison
- praising and cursing
- hypocrisy

Any of these concepts would make an interesting foundation for a learning activity. But that can create another problem—namely, how to decide which core concept(s) should be explored through a learning activity. After all, it might be fun to develop a small group meeting with eight distinct learning activities, but that wouldn't leave much room for anything else.

There are two ways to solve this potential problem. The first is to go broad and create a learning activity that addresses several core concepts at once. You can create one based on the "big idea," for example (which usually works well as an icebreaker).

The second solution is to choose a specific core concept based on need. Using the major concepts discovered in James 3:1-12, I may have created a learning activity that focused on "praising and cursing" if I felt my group members would be especially interested in that topic—or if I was using a prewritten curriculum that failed to address it.

As it happened, I chose the first solution. I decided to create a learning activity (an icebreaker, in this case) that would introduce the big idea at the beginning of the group meeting.

Step Two: Identify a Basic Activity

So, I wanted to create an icebreaker that highlighted the main theme for the group meeting: that the words we speak can accomplish powerful things for both good and evil. My next step was to come up with some kind of activity that could be connected to that theme.

I wish I could say there is a scientific method you can use for identifying these kinds of activities. But, in my experience at least, the process is all about brainstorming. It's a matter of mentally chewing on the theme you want to explore until something useful comes to mind.

Continuing the case study, my first instinct was to focus on words that can have both positive and negative meanings. Like when someone says, "That guy is bad to the bone!" It could be either a compliment or an insult. But I couldn't think of an activity to go along with that idea.

Then I became enamored of the idea of powerful words; the notion that words can carry a sense of heft and weight. I thought it would be fun to have my group members talk about words and phrases that had influenced them throughout the course of their lives—lines from a song, quotations from books or movies, words of wisdom spoken by a family member, and so on.

But it hit me that what I was thinking of only involved sitting and talking. I was close, but I wanted to create something that was more active—not a glorified discussion question.

In the end I decided to bring several newspapers and magazines to the group meeting. I would let my group members take a few copies and skim through them in search of powerful words. Then, after five minutes or so, we would go around the circle so that everyone could read whatever powerful words they had found.

Step Three: Add Layers as Needed

I've mentioned that learning activities are valuable because they appeal to people with different learning styles within a small group meeting. But that's not the only benefit that comes from their diverse nature; learning activities also stimulate the individual members of your group on different levels.

I think of this in terms of an athlete warming up his or her muscles. When I played football, for example, we would do a variety of drills at the beginning of every practice—jogging laps, Pilates, pushups, jumping jacks and so on. The purpose of these drills was to get blood flowing to our different muscle groups and stretch our tendons so that our bodies would be prepared for more intense exercise later in the practice.

In a similar way, learning activities can "warm up" small group participants on several different levels at the same time. Here are some examples of the different levels of experience that can be stimulated when a person participates in a robust learning activity:

Physical movement. It's a good idea to get your group members up and moving around every now and then. Americans spend a lot of time sitting down, which means an activity that requires movement can get your group members' blood flowing and help them wake up.

For example: Play a game of Simon Says and have your group members spin around, do jumping jacks, flap their arms and so on.

Intellectual awareness. You can use learning activities to help group members warm up their minds. This is especially helpful when your group tackles study material or portions of the Bible that are deep and require serious thought.

For example: Challenge your group members to solve a riddle, or divide the group into teams and have them race to finish a Sudoku puzzle.

Emotional awareness. Some group members need a little help when it comes to processing emotions around other people. (This is especially true for men.) You can provide that help by creating an activity that requires group members to tap into an emotional memory or situation.

For example: Have group members use crayons to draw a picture representing their last memory of a family member who passed away.

Spiritual awareness. Sometimes group leaders think that every element of a group meeting needs to be "spiritual." That isn't true—it's more than appropriate to play a game or talk about your favorite movies without Christianizing them. But it can be useful to help your group members extend their spiritual antennae during a group meeting.

For example: Incorporate elements of worship or prayer into a learning activity. Or have group members share their testimonies about coming to faith in Christ (as long as they feel comfortable doing so).

Relational awareness. If you don't have a fellowship time at the beginning of your group meetings, learning activities are a great way to strengthen the bonds of friendship between your group members. This should be done regularly.

For example: Lead the group in a team-building exercise, or play a social game like Apples to Apples or Taboo.

Creativity. Small groups often focus on information-based pursuits and activities. So it's a good idea to regularly use learning activities as an outlet for creativity. This will be appreciated by the members of your group who are more artistic and imaginative.

For example: Give each group member a tub of Play-Doh and have them make a sculpture representing faith. You could also split up into three smaller groups and have each group write a psalm expressing praise to God.

Curiosity. Curiosity may have killed the cat, but there is no doubt that it serves as an excellent motivator of human beings. Curious people are engaged people, which makes curiosity an important element of learning activities.

For example: Incorporate trivia questions into a learning activity, or learn a magic trick and see if your group members can figure out the secret.

Here's another public service announcement: You should not attempt to create a learning activity that engages all of these different levels of experience at once. That is not necessary and would not be helpful.

Rather, an effective learning activity will stimulate people on between two and four levels.

Mix and match. So, how does all of this fit into the task of creating an effective learning activity? Well, once you've settled on a basic structure for your learning activity, see if you can add one or more layers to the experience that will help participants warm up on more levels.

For example, look again at this unhelpful icebreaker question: What was your favorite color as a child? One of the reasons this is not effective as an icebreaker or learning activity is that its only real purpose is to get group members talking to each other. So, it stimulates people on a relational level and that's about it.

But what if you gave a ball to the first person answering the question, and then asked him or her to throw the ball to the person he or she wants to give an answer next? That would eliminate the predictable "going around the circle" bit, and it would also add some physical movement to the activity—another level of stimulation. You could take it a step further and have group members describe one of their happiest memories from childhood instead of their favorite color. That would add a level of emotional stimulation.

That's the basic idea—can I modify this activity so that it helps people become engaged in the group meeting on more and more levels?

Look again at the icebreaker activity I created for James 3. Giving my group members a chance to hunt through newspapers and magazines would stimulate their curiosity. Asking them to hunt for powerful words would stimulate them intellectually. And giving everyone a chance to read what they found (and explain why the words were powerful to them) would add in a level of relational engagement.

So, I had put together a robust activity—one that had the potential to stimulate my group members on several different levels.

After some thought, I did decide to add one more layer to the activity. I ended up bringing several pairs of scissors and instructed my group members to cut out whatever examples of powerful words they found. I thought we could put together a collage if we had time, which we didn't. But using the scissors did help everyone engage in more physical movement.

Step Four: Prepare for "Unpacking"

The final ingredient for any learning activity is a step that I call "unpacking" or "debriefing."

When you create a learning activity, you are trying to help your group members fully engage the Bible passage or study material you will be exploring together. You want them to become stimulated, to experience emotions and to grapple with core truths in a new and exciting way.

Unpacking allows participants to take a deep breath and process what they just experienced. It's a brief time for reflection—a time for everyone to think about their emotions and their reactions to the core truths that have been uncovered.

The actual process for unpacking involves two steps: asking questions and observation. The first you can prepare for prior to a group meeting, but the second is more spontaneous.

Asking questions. After deciding what you will ask group members to do during a learning activity, I recommend jotting down a quick set of questions that will help everyone debrief. Just like discussion questions help people create a dialogue connected to a Scripture passage or topic, the goal of these unpacking questions is to spark a conversation where participants can reflect on their experiences during the learning activity. This should not become a long list—between two and four questions is the ideal number.

When I write these questions, I think of squeezing a lemon wedge into a glass of water. The goal of the unpacking questions is to squeeze every last drop out of the learning activity—to pull out every insight and experience that can benefit the group.

For example, here are the unpacking questions I wrote for the learning activity about powerful words:

1. Which words found by other group members did you find to be especially powerful? Why?

2. From what source do you most often encounter powerful words?

3. When was the last time you wrote or spoke words that you considered to be powerful?

Notice that these questions refer back to what happened during the learning activity. But they also connect with the broader concepts addressed by that activity—in this case, the way that words have a powerful effect in our lives.

Observation. When it's time to actually lead your group through a learning activity, think of yourself as a small group anthropologist—be intentional about observing your group members as they participate. Specifically keep your eyes and ears open for two things: (1) group members who react strongly to the experience, and (2) actions or words that connect with the core concepts explored by the activity (including the "big idea").

If you were to lead the powerful-words activity, for example, you might see one of your group members writing down a quotation. Or someone might smile broadly or wince as he or she reads words considered powerful. You might hear a comment like, "I wish someone would say that about me."

When you observe these kinds of reactions—anything that indicates a person is experiencing something at a deeper level or interacting with a core concept—make a mental note of it. You may even want to write it down if you've got pen and paper handy. Then, bring it up again after the activity has ended.

Do this by stating what you observed and asking the group member if he or she wants to comment any further. "Sally, you were really beaming when you read that obituary. Was there anything in particular that made you feel happy?" Or, "Jim, what was it about that sentence that made you wish someone would say it to you?"

By doing this, you are giving group members a chance to open up and reveal something about themselves that is below the surface. The results can be surprising. I have seen people in my groups disclose new details of their story in response to such questions. I've also seen learning activities spark interesting discussions about difficult situations and even confessions of sin.

It's worth noting that some small group leaders aren't comfortable "calling out" their group members by name. I understand that. And, in general, it's best not to put people on the spot with questions they might not know how to answer. For example, you would not want to ask, "Jim, what other passages of Scripture talk about powerful words?"

Unpacking questions are different because you are simply asking group members to shed some light on the motivations behind their actions. It's not a matter of the person possibly getting a question wrong. It's a matter of whether or not a person is willing to reveal those motivations.

That brings up another important point: This is not a time for psychoanalyzing your group members. You should not try to draw out a person's thoughts with repeated questions, and you certainly should not try to force anyone to talk. You are simply observing a group member's reactions, stating what you observed, and then giving that group member a chance to reveal deeper *if he or she is ready*. If group members decline your invitation, or if they share something that stays on the surface, you move on. Period.

It's Not Cheating to Get Help

I firmly believe that anyone reading this book can create effective learning activities for their small groups. But that doesn't mean you should ignore help when it's available. There are a number of resources that provide prewritten icebreakers and learning activities—or, at the very least, quality activities that you can modify to fit your purposes.

My favorite option is SmallGroups.com, of course. The editors of that site have been collecting icebreakers and other group-based activities since 1998, which makes it the largest archive you can find online. The material is high quality, and the database is searchable—which is a big plus.

Whatever method you choose, be sure to harness the added energy and engagement that learning activities will bring to your small group meetings.

6

Crafting Great
Discussion Questions

There aren't a lot of things that make me really irritated, but one of them is tap water. The tap water in our home contained a bunch of extra minerals and particles, which means we weren't supposed to drink it. I know that's a pretty common problem in households across the country, and not being able to drink the water in and of itself isn't a big deal.

What bothers me is that we *should* be able to drink our tap water. In fact, we should be reveling in it!

Several years ago our city government had invested $22 million to build a state-of-the-art water purification and treatment plant just a few miles from our home. The facility is spread across forty acres of farmland and draws water primarily from a deep sandstone aquifer—not from Lake Michigan (which is an important detail in the suburbs of Chicago). It also features a top-of-the-line reverse osmosis system that distributes the water out into the community.

So, the water itself was not the problem. Every day we received gallons and gallons of the best water money can buy. There was no problem with our taps, either. My wife and I remodeled both the kitchen and the bathroom after we moved in, and we were sure to install high-quality sinks and spigots.

No, the trouble was with the pipes that provide the connection between our city's multimillion dollar treatment plant and our home's fancy faucets. Those pipes were old, for one thing, and most of them were iron. But several years back a previous owner had replaced a few of the pipes with copper. He meant well, I think, but he forgot to include a dielectric union between the old iron pipes and the new copper ones—which caused corrosion in several places.

The end result? When really good water sits in really bad pipes overnight, you get really bad water in your cup the next morning—no matter how new or clean your faucets are.

You may be experiencing something similar in your home— not with your tap water but with the dialogue and discussion in your small group.

Think about it. Just about every small group discussion starts with the best source material available: the Bible. Not only is it the bestselling book of all time, the Bible has literally changed the course of human history—and it was delivered by God himself, for crying out loud!

Plus, just about every small group discussion puts the Bible in the hands of interesting and intelligent people. Maybe you're thinking, *Well, you haven't met my small group members.* And that's true. But I'm willing to wager that every person in your group has a story to tell. And I'm willing to wager that the majority of your group members are capable of understanding what the Bible has to say and capable of putting it into practice throughout their lives.

So, if we have something interesting to discuss and interesting people to do the discussing, why are so many small group meetings uninteresting?

The answer, or at least one of the answers, is bad discussion questions. They are the pipes that usually connect group members with God's Word—and with each other. And if those pipes are bad, the discussion will probably be bad as well.

The Different Types of Discussion Questions

Before I became a homeowner, I had no idea that a typical American home contains several different kinds of pipes. There are pipes for water, pipes for gas and vent pipes just for air. Among those, you'll find pipes made of copper, iron and galvanized steel. There are also several kinds of plastic pipes, from PVC to PEX.

None of these materials is "better" than the others on a macrolevel. Rather, each type of pipe works best for a specific purpose. Taken all together they form a complex system that keeps our houses running smoothly.

There's a similar dynamic at play when it comes to discussion questions for your small group. You need to be aware that there are several types of questions, and you need to be aware of how each type works best within the context of your group.

To that end I'll spend the next few pages highlighting three broad patterns that discussion questions often follow. Then I will look at specific types of questions that reduce discussion and those that boost discussion, and how to put together an effective series of questions while preparing for a group meeting.

In doing so I will provide several example questions, all of which will be based on James 3:1-12.

Not many of you should presume to be teachers, my brothers, because you know that we who teach will be judged more strictly. We all stumble in many ways. If anyone is never at fault in what he says, he is a perfect man, able to keep his whole body in check.

When we put bits into the mouths of horses to make them obey us, we can turn the whole animal. Or take ships as an example. Although they are so large and are driven by strong winds, they are steered by a very small rudder wherever the pilot wants to go. Likewise the tongue is a small part of the body, but it makes great boasts. Consider what a great forest is set on fire by a small spark. The tongue also is a fire, a world of evil among the parts of the body. It corrupts the whole person, sets the whole course of his life on fire, and is itself set on fire by hell.

All kinds of animals, birds, reptiles and creatures of the sea are being tamed and have been tamed by man, but no man can tame the tongue. It is a restless evil, full of deadly poison.

With the tongue we praise our Lord and Father, and with it we curse men, who have been made in God's likeness. Out of the same mouth come praise and cursing. My brothers, this should not be. Can both fresh water and salt water flow from the same spring? My brothers, can a fig tree bear olives, or a grapevine bear figs? Neither can a salt spring produce fresh water.

Inductive questions. Studying the Bible has traditionally followed an inductive path made up of three steps: observing what the text says, interpreting what the text means and determining how the text can be applied. For that reason many modern Bible studies and curriculum guides use three major categories of questions: observation questions, interpretation questions and application questions.

Observation questions focus on finding out what the text says. They are straightforward and can almost always be answered by looking back into the Scripture passage or other material being discussed. For this reason observation questions are a good way to help your group identify information that will be useful later in the discussion. When used in moderation, they can also provide an easy way for people to chime in during a discussion.

Here are a few examples of observation questions:

- Why does James say that "not many" believers should become teachers?

- What images does James use to describe the effects of the tongue?

- What part of the body is small, but makes "great boasts"?

Interpretation questions focus on what the text means. They give group members an opportunity to dig below the surface and think about why the Holy Spirit inspired a certain passage to be written—to identify the themes, ideals, principles and commands it contains. Interpretation questions also provide an opportunity to explore things like textual context, historical context, word definitions and so on.

Here are a few examples of interpretation questions:

- What does James mean when he says that teachers will be "judged more strictly"?

- Do the works of the tongue always result in evil? Why or why not?

- What is the significance of fresh water and salt water flowing from the same stream?

Application questions explore how the text is relevant to my life—and how I can respond to it. These questions are personal and targeted, which means they often begin with something like "How can you . . ." or "What will we . . ." Their goal is to challenge group members to make a commitment or take some kind of action in their regular lives outside of the group.

Application questions work well when they have a direct connection with one or more interpretation questions from earlier in the discussion. Meaning, after group members decide what a specific Scripture text means, the best application questions encourage them to do something about it.

Here are a few examples of application questions:

- How can we remain humble when we attempt to teach and lead others?

- What are some ways to fix the damage caused by our speech?

- What steps are we willing to take in order to minimize hypocrisy within our group?

Open versus closed questions. Any question you can write for a small group meeting will fall into one of two camps: open or closed.

Closed questions are easy to identify because they only have one correct answer. Once that answer has been identified, another question or statement is required in order for the conversation to continue. For this reason closed questions should be used sparingly within a small group meeting. Too many of them will close the door on a meaningful discussion.

Still, I am not advocating that closed questions be totally eliminated from small group meetings; they can be useful in certain situations. For example, they are an effective way to officially introduce a topic or piece of information into a discussion. They also can be helpful as a way to set up other questions that are better suited for sparking a conversation.

Here are two examples:

- What is the source of the "fire" contained within the tongue? (Introduces the topic of hell.)

- Can a fig tree bear olives? (Sets up the next question: How is it possible for followers of Jesus to produce harmful fruit with their words?)

Open questions are the opposite of closed questions in that they have several possible answers—none of which are necessarily right or wrong. For this reason you want to focus on open questions as you prepare for a small group meeting. Their presence will open the door to long and meaningful discussions.

"How is it possible for followers of Jesus to produce harmful fruit with their words?" is a good example of an open question. There is no single correct answer, and it can be explored from several different angles.

Text-based versus experience-based questions. A third pattern often present in Bible studies and curriculum guides is the movement from text-based questions to questions that are based on personal experience.

Text-based questions are focused on whatever source material is being studied by the group—a passage of Scripture, a book, a speaker on a DVD, a movie and so forth. These questions shine a spotlight on that source material, allowing the group to dissect and debate its contents. Therefore the discussions produced by these questions are usually impersonal and clinical; they are focused on the text rather than the group members themselves.

On the other side of the coin are personal-experience questions, which are focused on group members—their history and life experiences—instead of an "outside" text. The conversations produced by these questions are relational and sometimes deeply personal. Such questions are an important element in small group meetings because they give group members a chance to share more about their stories.

Here are some examples of experience-based questions:

- What are some common characteristics of teachers who have made a positive impact in your life?

- What circumstances usually result in you losing control of your tongue?

- How do you react when you are confronted by hypocrisy in another person?

Mix and match. One reason I've highlighted these different patterns among discussion questions is to give you a sense of the options you have when preparing for a small group meeting. There are many types of questions that can be asked, and being familiar with these patterns will help you achieve diversity in the questions you select.

Diversity is an important word when it comes to discussion questions. Having read through hundreds of Bible studies and curriculum guides in recent years, I've noticed that too many of them fall into common (and stale) routines.

A lot of studies are basically workbooks, for example. They are filled with closed observation questions—sometimes in the form of fill-in-the-blank sentences—punctuated by two or three application questions at the end. These guides work well for recording information and regurgitating doctrine, but they do little to produce actual discussion.

Other studies follow a strict inductive pattern. This starts with a large dose of observation questions (most of them closed), followed by several interpretation questions. Again, application questions are at the end. This is an efficient way to explore a passage of Scripture or a chapter in a book; however, these questions rarely move away from a text-based exploration and toward the experiences and stories of the people involved in the discussion.

I have found that by mixing and matching the different patterns of questions listed earlier, you can add a richness and depth to your discussion experiences that is missing when all of the questions feel the same, or when the group follows the same routine week after week. So be creative. Be diverse.

If you've written four interpretation questions in a row, add a question in the middle that allows group members to take a breather and talk about their personal experiences. Throw out an application question at the beginning of a discussion rather than always waiting until the end. (By the way, you might be surprised at how attempting to apply a truth will aid in the understanding of that truth.)

Questions That Kill Discussion

I mentioned earlier that closed questions have the potential to "close the door" on a meaningful discussion. Alas, they are not the only ones. There are several different types of questions that can kill almost any discussion in just about any small group. I've listed some of the most common below.

Idiot questions. These are questions that have extremely obvious answers—so obvious that only an idiot could get them wrong.[14] Unfortunately, many small group leaders are fond of these types of questions. The thinking is that such questions will get people talking because everyone already knows the answer—thus sparking a discussion like kindling in a fire.

The reality is that people aren't comfortable giving the answer to an obvious question. The idea of verbalizing something that everyone already knows makes people feel silly (or even idiotic). As a result, idiot questions are usually followed by a long bout of awkward silence and sheepish glances—until someone blurts out the answer in an effort to cut the rising tension. This effect is compounded when several idiot questions occur together.

Here are a couple examples:

- What do we put in the mouths of horses to make them obey us?
- Is it true that no human being can tame the tongue?

Unreasonable questions. These questions fall at the opposite end of the spectrum in that their answers are unreasonably complicated or obscure. These are questions that no one in the group will be able to answer unless they speak Hebrew or have access to a biblical commentary. Unreasonable questions often make their way into a small group discussion when group leaders spend a lot of time in preparation and get a little overzealous about what they've learned.

For example: How would a first-century interpretation of the word *tongue* impact our understanding of this passage?

Long-winded questions. Sometimes the structure of a discussion question—the way it's written or the way it's asked—can result in confusion among small group members. This often happens when someone attempts to squeeze a lot of information into a question, causing it to be overly long, or when a question requires some extra explanation in order to be understood.

As with unreasonable questions, long-winded questions are often the byproduct of overzealous preparation on the part of the small group leader. In reality, people find it very difficult to engage in a discussion when they don't understand what is being asked of them.

Here's an example of a long-winded question: How do verses 11-12, which are rhetorical questions—a common literary device used in James's day—impact our understanding of the principle outlined in verses 9-10?

I want to make it clear that providing extra information to your group members is not always a bad thing. But when you find yourself in a situation where some context would be useful for your group members, I recommend just telling it to them in a straightforward way before you ask the next question.

For example: Rhetorical questions were a common literary device in James's day, and he uses three of them in verses 11-12. How do these questions impact our understanding of verses 9-10?

Compound questions. Compound questions are a variation of long-winded questions. Instead of packing a lot of information into a single query, group leaders will sometimes stack three or more questions together, rapid-fire, when those questions address a similar subject. What usually happens in these situations is that someone will answer the last question in the series, and the preceding questions will be largely ignored.

Here's an example of a compound question: How does it make you feel to hear that teachers will be judged more strictly? Why do you feel that way? What qualifications for teachers are listed elsewhere in Scripture?

The solution is simply to break the string of questions apart and ask them one at a time.

"Leading the witness" questions. Some discussion questions are phrased in such a way that it's obvious the group leader is seeking a specific answer, or that the group leader wants to steer the discussion in a specific direction. This is a bad idea for several reasons, not the least of which is the lack of respect demonstrated toward the other participants in the discussion. Group leaders who ask these kinds of questions behave like sheep dogs attempting to herd other people toward their way of thinking.

The bottom line is this: Be wary of questions that contain any kind of built-in opinions.

For example: Does it seem like James is using hyperbole in verse 6, and what is his purpose in doing so?

The best way to fix "leading the witness" questions is to be honest about your opinions. (Even though you are the small group leader, you are still allowed to share what you think.)

An easy fix. The good thing about bad questions is that they are easy to remedy. If you are writing a study from scratch, don't allow any of these insidious queries to creep into your material. To help with that, it's always good to perform a second edit on your work before the group gets together.

And if you find these kinds of questions in a prewritten Bible study, use a pen to scratch them out before the first group member even walks through your door. Remember: you hold the key to eliminating discussion-killing questions from your small group.

Questions That Boost Discussion

All right—enough about content that needs to be excluded from your small group meetings. There are several types of questions that can produce a positive impact within a group discussion. I've already mentioned two: open questions and experience-based questions. Fortunately, there are several more.

As before, all example questions will be based on James 3:1-12.

Emotional questions. One way to avoid a discussion that focuses too much on the transfer of information is to include discussion questions that help people tap into their feelings and emotions. Such questions don't have to be overly sentimental or dramatic—in fact, they shouldn't be. You just need to be sure that from time to time you are asking people to consider what they are feeling in addition to asking what they know.

For example: How do you react to the claim in verse 2 that "we all stumble in many ways"?

Thoughtful questions. I first heard about the "five minute rule" from Kevin Miller when he was a vice president at Christianity Today International. Kevin was giving a presentation to all of the editors on our team when he said: "If an article comes across your desk, ask yourself: *Could an average reader write of this on their own if they explored the topic for five minutes?*"

That's the "five minute rule," and I have found it to be very helpful both as an editor and a small group leader. I'm not saying that every discussion question you put before your group should be deeply thought-provoking or provocative. But some of them should be. After all, the goal of gathering as a group is to encounter God's Spirit in life-changing ways, and that usually doesn't happen when you keep things at the surface.

Here are a couple examples of thoughtful questions:

- Keeping in mind James's warning from verse 1, read 1 Timothy 1:3-11. How can believers know that they are ready and able to become spiritual teachers?

- How much control can a human being gain over his or her tongue this side of eternity?

Controversial questions. First, a note of caution: getting people stirred up to the point of arguing may result in an active discussion, but it rarely produces positive results—especially in terms of creating an atmosphere conducive to spiritual growth. So it's best to avoid asking contentious questions merely as a way to get people talking.

Still, controversial questions should have a place in your small group meetings. That's because God's Word addresses several issues that are vital to the Christian life—things like sin, salvation, miracles, money and gender—and yet people don't always agree on what the Bible says regarding these issues. They are controversial topics, and helping your group explore them is part of honestly addressing the text.

Here's an example of a question that is both controversial and helpful: Is it acceptable for followers of Jesus to denounce the sins of others? Why or why not?

Follow-up questions. Small group leaders are often told that they need to be good at *facilitating* the discussions and interactions between their group members. That's an academic word, but all it really boils down to is knowing how to provide a spark or a little grease to your group's discussion when things begin to stall. And one of the best ways to serve as a facilitator is to ask follow-up questions.

These are spontaneous questions that a group leader uses to get clarification about a statement from a group member, to ask for more information, to seek out an illustration or to open a topic up to the other people in the group.

Here are a few examples of follow-up questions:

- Dave, I hear you saying that James is using hyperbole throughout these verses. Does everyone agree with that idea?

- What makes you say that moving away from sarcasm was the hardest thing you've ever done?

- Susan, you mentioned that verses 11-12 are full of rhetorical questions. Is that important?

Creating an Effective Series of Discussion Questions

The remainder of this chapter will address how to put together a series of discussion questions during the process of writing your own material. But I want to start with a few thoughts about tweaking the discussion questions you find in a prewritten or published Bible study.

First and foremost, you need to cut out whatever material doesn't fit with your small group. And that definitely includes discussion questions.

The vast majority of printed Bible studies I have seen contain way more discussion questions than a group would be able to address and answer in a single gathering—and that's on purpose. (I'll address this further in chapter eight.) It's your job to pick and choose the questions that will be best suited for your group. Of course, if you come across any of the discussion-killing questions mentioned earlier, get rid of them.

After you have cut out any unnecessary discussion questions, see if there are any holes that need to be filled in. Will any of the remaining questions approach your group members at an emotional level? Will they help your group members interact with and share their own stories? Are there any deep, thoughtful questions? If not, you should probably add in a few questions to balance things out.

Your most important discussion question. I've mentioned several types and patterns of questions in this chapter. Most of them have value in the context of a small group discussion. And yet I don't use any of them to start discussions in the small group meetings I lead. That's because I always use the same question to begin a small group discussion—a question that I believe is more important and useful than any other.

Here is what I say to my group members to get things started: "I want to get your initial reactions to the Scripture passage we'll be discussing in this gathering. What was surprising or significant or confusing about the text as you read it through?" (Of course, I use different phrases if the group will be focusing on a specific topic or the chapter of a book, rather than a Scripture passage.)

So many small group leaders feel like they have to anticipate how their group members will react to a particular topic or section of the Bible in order to write effective discussion questions. Or they feel like they need to come up with a series of universal questions that will be universally interesting to each person in the group.

But stop and think about that for a moment. Isn't it a bit arrogant to expect our group members to talk for thirty to ninety minutes about the topics and questions that we, the group leaders, find most compelling? At the least, it's biting off more than we can chew.

In my opinion it's much simpler (and much more effective) to allow those group members to express what they find interesting or confusing or significant—and then follow that discussion as far as it will take you.

Of course, what your group members want to talk about might be different from the discussion topics and questions you had planned. But that's okay. It's more than okay, right? The whole point of gathering as a group is to interact with God's Word and each other in a way that creates life-changing experiences. And if that means letting go of what you had planned to talk about— so be it.

The only exception is when the group is moving far away from what you had identified as the "big idea." When that happens, you need to make a decision on the fly: will you go with the flow and allow the group to determine the main topic, or will you rein in the discussion and return to your original "big idea"? That's a decision that needs to be made in the moment, and you'll have to trust your instincts and experience to make it.

I realize that taking this approach assumes your group members will read through the Bible passages or source material before the group gets together. And maybe you're thinking: *that won't happen with my group!* There is an easy way to fix this. I've found that reading the passage out loud as a group before the discussion starts is a great way to solve this problem—and a great habit to form anyway.

Free write the next set of questions. Okay, now that you have your first (and most important) discussion question figured out, it's time to come up with some more. The best way to go about this is to write down every question that pops into your mind as you read through the Scripture passage or other material under discussion.

This is similar to a technique called "free writing" that writers often use to get their brains working (or to fix a bout of writer's block). In free writing, you write down whatever comes into your head for a set period of time. The idea is to begin the mechanical process of writing, which helps trigger other brain functions like creativity, problem solving and so on.

So try some free writing with your discussion questions. Read through the Bible verses a few times and just jot down any question that pops into your mind. Don't be picky here and don't try to weed out questions that won't work for the discussion—that comes later. This is just brainstorming.

Identify the stress points. The next step is to search for what I call the "stress points" within the text. These are the words and phrases that address weightier topics and ideas—the meat of a Scripture passage. In other words, these are the portions of the text that seem most interesting and important both for positive and negative reasons.

Positive stress points are words and phrases that provide explanations or highlight important truths. They may include:

- *Doctrinal statements.* Some passages of Scripture serve as the basis or explanation for key doctrines of the Christian faith. These provide a great opportunity for education, discussion and growth. For example, Ephesians 2:8-9 serves as a scriptural foundation for the doctrine of salvation by grace: "For it is by grace you have been saved, through faith—and this not from yourselves, it is the gift of God—not by works, so that no one can boast."

- *Commands.* Because obedience and application are such important elements for spiritual growth, God-inspired commands recorded in the pages of Scripture are a great stopping point for discussion. Romans 12 contains a number of commands, for example, including verse 14: "Bless those who persecute you; bless and do not curse."

  One of the things that makes commands great material for small group discussion is that we usually need to do a bit of digging before we understand who the command applies to. Are all Christians commanded to "bless those who persecute you," for example? Or was that only for the early Christians in Rome who received Paul's letter? That's a useful spark for conversation.

- *Promises.* As with commands, when we discover a Spirit-inspired promise within the pages of Scripture, we should pay attention. Look at Matthew 17:20, for example: "I tell you the truth, if you have faith as small as a mustard seed, you can say to this mountain, 'Move from here to there,' and it will move. Nothing will be impossible for you." Again, that's a great launching pad for discussion because it requires us to identify who is being addressed in addition to what is being said.

- *Visual elements.* Our culture is very visual, and so the visual elements embedded in Scripture passages will likely stand out to your group members—things like word pictures, metaphors, visions, poetic descriptions and so on.

Negative stress points are verses or passages of Scripture that may cause confusion or controversy within your group's discussion. They could include:

- *Confusing words and phrases.* There are many Bible translations available today, and many commentaries and other resources that help us understand what biblical texts say and mean. Even so, a number of confusing passages remain. Like these verses from 1 Peter 3:19-20, which involve Jesus: "After being made alive, he went and made proclamation to the imprisoned spirits—to those who were disobedient long ago when God waited patiently in the days of Noah while the ark was being built" (NIV 2011). Chances are good that at least a few group members will become stuck on a passage like that, which makes it a great stopping point for group discussion.

- *Controversial texts.* Some texts are more controversial than confusing. Different camps believe strongly in different interpretations and applications. A good example is 1 Timothy 2:12: "I do not permit a woman to teach or to have authority over a man; she must be silent." Some people feel very strongly that this command applies to all women in the church throughout all time; others feel strongly that this is limited to a specific culture (or even a specific church). There are sharp lines drawn, and that makes for controversy.

  Be careful when you address controversial topics and Bible passages, however, because they carry the potential to produce frustration, bitterness and even anger. People are more apt to fight about something when there is a well-defined disagreement, rather than confusion.

- *Boring passages of Scripture.* It's true; there are many people who find sections of the Bible to be boring—those long lists in the book of Numbers, for example, or the genealogy of Jesus in Matthew 1. And yet, strangely, those passages still have great potential for discussion within a small group. That's because they allow you to ask the question, *Why?* Why does the author include all of these lists? Why does the same phrase keep repeating over and over? Why does Matthew spend so much effort making a connection between Jesus and Abraham?

It's exciting when a group can start identifying answers to some of these questions—like an archaeologist discovering valuable treasures in what looked at first like a pile of sand. That being said, sometimes you need to provide some outside information in order to spark those discoveries. So have a commentary or study notes available when you are preparing for a group meeting that will cover potential boring material.

Continuing the case study, here are a few stress points I would identify from James 3:1-12:

- Verse 1 contains a promise, albeit a negative one: "we who teach will be judged more strictly."

- Verse 1 is also potentially confusing. (What qualifies someone as a "teacher," for example? And why will teachers be judged more strictly?)

- Verses 3-12 contain several visual elements, including metaphors (comparing the tongue with a rudder or with a fire) and strong images (horses, a ship, fire, several animals, springs of water and so on).

Again, chances are good that your group members will zero in on one or more of these stress points during their own reading of the text—which means these topics are good material for discussion.

So, check back over your brainstormed list of questions and see if any of them connect with the stress points you've identified. If so, you should give them strong consideration when you finalize your list of questions. And review the stress points to see if they spark other discussion questions you had not previously considered, and add those to the list.

Filter questions through the big idea. Once you've got a good list of questions, use the "big idea" for the group meeting as a way to winnow out any questions that don't support the main theme or idea you hope to explore. I do this by crossing out questions that have no connection with the "big idea."

For example, here is a brainstormed list of questions based on James 3:1-12:

- Why will believers who teach be judged more strictly?

- What are some of the "many ways" you stumble in your walk as a Christian?

- Is it true that no human being can tame the tongue?

- How much control can a human being gain over his or her tongue this side of eternity?

- Is James using hyperbole in verse 6, or is he speaking truthfully?

- Can the tongue be used for good as well as evil?

- Is it acceptable for followers of Jesus to denounce the sins of others? Why or why not?

- What songs or hymns are most effective in helping you connect with God?

- What does it mean that human beings are created in "God's likeness" (v. 9)?

- How do you interpret James's use of rhetorical questions in verses 11-12?

Here is the "big idea" I had established for the group meeting: *the words we speak can accomplish powerful things both for good and evil.* When I eliminate the questions that don't support that idea, I get the following:

- ~~Why will believers who teach be judged more strictly?~~

- ~~What are some of the "many ways" you stumble in your walk as a Christian?~~

- Is it true that no human being can tame the tongue?

- How much control can a human being gain over his or her tongue this side of eternity?

- Is James using hyperbole in verse 6, or is he speaking truthfully?

- Can the tongue be used for good as well as evil?

- Is it acceptable for followers of Jesus to denounce the sins of others? Why or why not?

- ~~What songs or hymns are most effective in helping you connect with God?~~

- ~~What does it mean that human beings are created in "God's likeness" (v. 9)?~~

- How do you interpret James's use of rhetorical questions in verses 11-12?

Finalize your list of questions. Here's an important piece of advice: Don't try to incorporate too many questions into your final plan. A good rule of thumb is to write between five and ten questions for every hour your group will spend in discussion. That may not seem like enough, but think about it—answering ten questions in a period of an hour means that each question would only receive six minutes of attention from the entire group.

It's much better to explore the most important questions deeply than to take a shotgun approach and try to cover a whole spread of questions in a shallow way.

After the preceding steps, you should have several questions that will work well in your upcoming small group meeting. The final step is to pick out the ones you believe have the most potential for sparking and maintaining a meaningful discussion.

To cut down your list of questions, start by making sure there are no discussion-killing questions remaining. If so, try to find a way to rewrite or edit them so they can be more effective. If they are just bad questions, let them go. If you still have too many questions, you need to make a judgment call—which questions will be most helpful for your specific group?

For example, here is the final list of questions I prepared for my small group meeting on James 3:1-12:

- What did you find surprising or significant or confusing about these verses?

- What are the primary images James uses in this passage, and how do you react to them?

- As you are comfortable, talk about moments from your past that support James's claim in verse 8: "[The tongue] is a restless evil, full of deadly poison."

- In what ways can the tongue be used for good?

- In which of these verses (if any) do you believe James is speaking hyperbolically?

- How much control can a human being gain over his or her tongue this side of eternity?

- How do you interpret James's use of rhetorical questions in verses 11-12?

- What steps can we take to minimize the damage caused by the tongue within this small group?

Before I move on to the topic of incorporating worship and prayer in a small group meeting, let me mention one last thing: this process of crafting great discussion questions for your small group does not have to be time consuming, complicated or difficult. In fact, it can become second nature—given a little practice and concentration.

As you think deeply about the discussion questions you present to your small group, you will more easily recognize those that boost or kill conversations within each meeting. And the more you go through the process of free writing discussion questions, working with stress points and winnowing out the best material, the easier that process will become.

7

Planning for
Worship and Prayer

It's happened dozens of times during my tenure as a small group leader. I'll be in the middle of facilitating a spirited discussion when I glance at the clock and realize, with a jolt, that I should have dismissed the group ten minutes ago.

It's not that going ten minutes over is a big deal. Rather, what causes that jolt is the realization that I still have more elements I want the group to experience—more of the essential activities I had planned on incorporating into the meeting.

For me, the essential activities that get left behind most often are worship and prayer. And judging by the e-mails I have received over the years, I'm not the only one who experiences this on a regular basis. Indeed, I've read many notes from small group leaders asking how they can manage time within their group meetings so that worship and prayer don't get left behind. And I've received many more e-mails from small group pastors who want advice on how to make worship and prayer a greater priority for their group leaders.

Fortunately, small group leaders can take two steps to avoid regularly neglecting worship and prayer in their group meetings.

First, don't wait until the end of each group meeting to engage in worship and prayer. Maybe that sounds obvious, but I've drifted into a rut many times when it comes to the way I structure each small group meeting. And it doesn't help that most prewritten Bible studies follow a predictable pattern: icebreaker, discussion, an application question, then worship and prayer.

I recommend shaking things up as you prepare for your group meetings over time. It's a great idea to start a meeting with prayer, for example. Or to lead a worship activity in the middle of a series of discussion questions. Or to spend an entire group meeting in worship and prayer (every now and then).

Second, don't settle for a generic view of worship and prayer. Worship can be more than breaking out a guitar and singing a few songs. Prayer should include more than going around in a circle and taking requests. When you plan worship and prayer activities that are more robust and diversified, your group members will respond in a more positive way—and you'll have an easier time featuring those activities in your group meetings.

With that in mind, here are several strategies that can help you make full-bodied plans for worship and prayer within your small group meetings.

Planning for Worship

My son Daniel is a huge fan of the movie *How to Train Your Dragon,* and he was delighted to receive a miniature "Night Fury" dragon as a recent Christmas gift. If you haven't seen that particular film, picture a sleek, jet-black reptile with the wings of a bat and the eyes of a crocodile. (Yeah, it's a pretty cool toy.)

The neat thing is that Daniel's Night Fury is an exact replica of the dragon from the movie—it has all of the same markings and features, just condensed into a package that is smaller and safer.

Keep that image in mind, because I'm afraid that's what many of us attempt to do with worship in our small groups—create a miniature replica of Sunday mornings that is smaller and safer.

It's an easy temptation to embrace because so many people enjoy the thrill of worship on Sunday mornings. We like being carried away by a sea of voices and musical instruments, all praising God in unison. We also like the convenience of a Power-Point display all queued up to lead us through the verses and repeating choruses.

So when it comes time to worship in our small groups, we try to imitate that kind of atmosphere. But more often than not we end up robbing our worship experiences of their power.

The problem, of course, is that the worship setting in a small group is much different from what happens on Sunday mornings. There is no band. There is no staff member or layperson spending hours in preparation for the worship set. There are no PowerPoint slides or specially produced videos.

And that's okay. Your small group is an intimate gathering where a few people can assemble and seek to encounter God together. It's a different atmosphere for worship, not better or worse. Jesus said, "For where two or three come together in my name, there am I with them" (Matthew 18:20), not "Whenever everyone gets together on Sunday morning."

That being the case, here are several activities and practices that can help you embrace the intimacy of small group worship:

- *Pray early and often.* The purpose of worship is to connect with and praise God in a deep, meaningful way. And nothing facilitates that kind of experience like prayer—especially when a small group of Christians can focus together on seeking the Lord in unison.

- *Scripture and prayer readings.* Prewritten readings based on Scripture can be powerful as a group worship activity. Give people a chance to read God's Word out loud, and be sure to include moments of silence that allow those words to soak in. You can also find several books containing prayers and exhortations to God (similar to the Psalms), most of which are a great way to express worship and devotion. One time-tested example is the Book of Common Prayer.

- *Object lessons.* Consider leading a worship activity based on a concrete image or object lesson. Have group members hold candles in a darkened room, for example, or ask them to write some of their fears on slips of paper and nail them to a wooden cross. These activities often help people experience an abstract concept in a new and more emotive way. (You can find several examples of object lessons and other activities on SmallGroups.com.)

- *Take Communion.* Jesus instituted the practice of Communion during a dinner with twelve of his closest friends. Referring back to that event, Paul gave these instructions to Jesus' followers: "*whenever* you eat this bread and drink this cup, you proclaim the Lord's death until he comes" (1 Corinthians 11:26, emphasis added). That gives you a great opportunity to worshipfully lead your group members in a time of remembering Christ's sacrifice and resurrection.

  It should be noted that some church and denominational leaders may not look favorably on a small group practicing Communion. And if that's the case in your church culture, you probably don't want to make waves over the issue. There are other ways to worship, after all.

- *Sing some songs!* I certainly don't want to imply that singing is not an appropriate form of worship for a small group. It is, and singing together as a group can be powerful. But singing should not be your group's only form of worship, and it should be tailored for a group setting. Give an opportunity for requests, for example. Or let multiple people take the lead from song to song.

Remember, embrace worship in your small group as a chance to connect with God—and the other members of your group—in an intimate setting.

Planning for Prayer

The most frustrated I have ever felt in a small group meeting was during a prayer time several years ago. Things started out badly when we went around the circle to share requests. It seemed like every person in the group shared at least one request that was completely tangential—their uncle's neighbor was thinking about a career change, or someone at work had done something silly and offended other people at work.

When the time came to actually start praying, I made a big mistake. "I'll open us in prayer," I said. "Who is willing to close?" There was silence for at least thirty seconds—complete with people awkwardly looking at the ceiling or their own toes—and I mentally kicked myself for even asking the question. Finally, mercifully, my wife volunteered to close, and we got rolling.

I was already feeling distracted at this point, so my opening salvo was pretty generic. "Lord, we're thankful that you've helped us gather here safely tonight. Please bless us as we bring our requests to you." Other group members continued in that vein—regurgitating different requests and sometimes throwing in bits of advice for good measure.

One guy in particular got my blood boiling. He prayed for several minutes straight, and he kept tossing around clichés and jargon phrases like rice at a wedding. I remember thinking, *Somebody needs to teach this guy how to pray.*

And then it hit me: that somebody was me. I was the one charged with teaching this guy how to pray. In fact, I was charged with leading the whole group in meaningful, productive times of prayer. And I had failed.

In recent years I've learned several strategies for facilitating a fruitful prayer experience during a small group meeting. (And I will share many of those strategies in chapter ten.) But I've also determined that group leaders need to take an important step of preparation *before* each group meeting.

Specifically, group leaders need to plan diverse prayer experiences that are meaningful within the context of each group meeting. In other words, we need to put some time and effort into thinking about how to pray differently for different group meetings. It's okay to "go around the circle" with prayer requests every now and then, but if that's the only method we use for group prayer, the group will be in danger of falling into a rut.

So, here are several ideas for prayer activities that can be tailored to your group as you prepare for specific group meetings:

- *Concert prayer.* This technique is as simple as it is revolutionary. Everyone goes around the circle and talks about their prayer requests, and then everyone prays for those requests together. Out loud. At the same time. Your group literally becomes a symphony of prayer as everyone lifts their voices and their supplications together in unison.

  Having tried this in several small groups, I can say that your group members may feel a little self-conscious about this at first—maybe even a little uncomfortable. But trust me when I say that they will start to see the benefits after a few repetitions. The unity your group will experience through this chorus of prayer is wonderful, and people will no longer feel worried about saying something silly because nobody else is listening.

- *Immediate prayer.* With this technique, the group prays for a person immediately after he or she shares their prayer requests and areas of praise. For example, if Rob notes three things he would like the group to pray for, the group stops right there and prays for each of Rob's requests. Then the same thing happens with the next person, and so on. (It's not important for every single group member to pray for every single request; people can pray as they feel led.)

This way group members don't have to sift through all of the requests for the entire group when it comes time to actually pray. You don't have to concentrate on remembering everything, so you can concentrate on praying and agreeing with others who pray. (As a side note, the group can pray in a "normal" fashion for each person's requests, or it can use the concert-prayer method.)

- *Subgrouping.* This is a variation of the two previous techniques where the group divides into three or four subgroups in order to facilitate the process of prayer. These groups can be random (pick the two people on your right) or specific (men gather with other men). Again, the idea is to make it easier for group members to concentrate on each other and on the process of praying without feeling the weight of being responsible for the entire group at all times.

- *Themed prayer.* The idea here is to pick a theme on which your group will concentrate its prayers for a particular session. Options for themes include troubles or blessings your group members are experiencing at work, fears that people are struggling with, family prayers and praises, and so on.

- *Segmented prayer.* You may have heard someone break prayer down into four different components: adoration, confession, thanksgiving and supplication. (This is often referred to in acronym form as the ACTS of prayer or a prayer CAST.) In segmented prayer, a group focuses on one of these components for an individual group meeting. So, this method is similar to themed prayer, except the group focuses on a specific aspect of prayer rather than a theme of prayer requests.

Of course, these are not the only activities you can use as you prepare to lead others in prayer. Read, explore, experiment and build a system of prayer that is best suited for your small group.

Remember the "Big Idea"

As with icebreakers, it's common for prayer and worship to be viewed as separate from the learning activities within a small group meeting. A group may engage in discussion and application around a specific theme, but that theme is dropped when the time comes for prayer or worship at the end of a meeting. This way of thinking has been echoed by several small group leaders I've spoken with over the years, and it's prevalent in many of the prewritten Bible studies available today.

But such a separation is unnatural. If the primary goal of a small group meeting is spiritual growth and transformation, then participants need to do more than engage in discussion around the truths found in God's Word. They need to respond to those truths. And worship and prayer (in addition to application) are great ways to help your group members begin such a response.

So here is my advice: as often as you can, make a connection between the activities you choose for prayer and worship and the "big idea" of your group meeting. You can also make connections with specific verses or themes explored in the group meeting that fall under the umbrella of the "big idea."

Continuing the case study on James 3:1-12, remember that I had come up with this as my "big idea": *the words we speak can accomplish powerful things both for good and evil.*

There were several worship activities that would have fit well with this theme. The most obvious would have been to invite everyone to use our tongues for good by singing songs of praise (or maybe reading through the lyrics together). I also could have found a responsive reading that addresses the power of the tongue.

Or I could have taken a different route and led the group in a time of silent contemplation and worship. (It would have been fun to pass out tongue depressors for such an experience as an object lesson.)

In the end, I chose to lead the group in reading Psalm 145 out loud, which ends with this verse:

> My mouth will speak in praise of the LORD.
>   Let every creature praise his holy name
>   for ever and ever.

Leading a time of concert prayer would have been a great choice for a prayer activity to fit my "big idea" for James 3:1-12. I could have also divided the group into smaller clusters and asked each subgroup to pray through a different psalm.

I decided to try a segmented prayer where we focused on the confession of sin. Specifically, I asked the group to consider confessing times when their speech had hurt another person or misrepresented what a follower of God should be. It was a somber experience, but beneficial—and a great way to respond to James's admonition that using our tongues for evil "should not be."

8

Finalizing Curriculum

I'm not a fan of male stereotypes in general, but there is one in particular that gets me fired up: the idea that men don't ask for directions. I get irritated whenever I hear that because I am positively a man, and I am also a big fan of asking for directions. Whether it's gas station attendants or people walking their dogs, if I'm lost, I will find somebody who can get me back on the right track.

Actually, what I really like is to carry directions with me so that I don't get lost in the first place. In fact, before the GPS revolution, it was common for me to put together detailed folders for our family road trips—complete with printed sheets for driving directions, hotel information, landmarks and more.

I think it's important for small group leaders to take a similar approach with their group meetings. And that's where curriculum comes in.

That word *curriculum* carries different meanings for different people. But in the context of a small group, it really just means a plan for the different activities a group will experience in the short term (a single small group meeting) and long term (a six-week curriculum on the book of James). Incidentally, many small group practitioners have started referring to the activities within a single gathering as an "agenda" or "meeting plan," which is a helpful distinction (and one that I will use at times throughout this chapter).

So, your final step in preparing for a small group meeting should be to put together a finished plan that helps you navigate the different activities you want to experience with your group. And that is true whether you are using a prewritten curriculum or have come up with everything yourself.

Finalizing Prewritten Curriculum

My wife is an excellent cook, and she prefers to make all of her preparations from scratch when she can. But now that we have two young boys running around the house, she's forced to take a few shortcuts every now and then.

For example, one of my favorite meals is a mandarin orange chicken that she buys from Trader Joe's. The chicken is frozen, and Jess heats it in the oven for eighteen minutes. While it's cooking, she defrosts the two packets of sauce that are included and cooks up a cup of basmati rice. After she pulls the chicken out of the oven, she stirs in the sauce and puts everything back for another two minutes. Then she throws it on a plate with the rice and dribbles some extra sauce over the top. Next comes a really nice salad with spring greens, baby spinach, walnuts, dried cherries, sunflower seeds and some balsamic vinaigrette. The last touch is a cold glass of reverse-osmosis-filtered water.

Voila! She puts it all on the table while I gather the children, and we all have a great experience.

I want you to keep that image in mind over the next few pages, because it's a useful picture as you think about using prewritten Bible studies in your small group. They are a great tool that have the potential to be spiritually nourishing for you and the other members of your community. But you never want to experience them straight out of the bag.

Fortunately, customizing a prewritten Bible study to fit the needs of your group only takes two steps: (1) Cut any material that doesn't fit with your "big idea," and (2) add in supplemental material if necessary.

Cutting Material

This may surprise you: it's just as important for you to identify a "big idea" when using a prewritten study as it is when you write a study from scratch. That's because a big idea is the best tool at your disposal for getting rid of unnecessary material.

Do you remember those octagonal toys that every household in America has owned at one point or another? The ones with cutouts of different shapes on each side, and the kids have a blast sliding triangles or ovals or stars through the correct cutout and then dumping everything back on the floor? Well, that's a great image for how the "big idea" works as you finalize your agenda for a small group meeting.

When you identify a "big idea" for a particular study, it's like you are choosing a shape on that toy. (Let's say a triangle for the purposes of this illustration.) From that moment on, you are going to get rid of anything in the study that doesn't fit through the triangle-shaped hole—anything that doesn't fit smoothly and easily into your "big idea."

Maybe you feel uncomfortable with the idea of messing with a published Bible study. Maybe you don't feel confident in your ability to make the right decisions, or maybe you feel like you should stick with what the expert has planned.

Well, I have written a good deal of curriculum in recent years, and I have edited quite a bit more. So hear me when I say this: just about every piece of prewritten curriculum you will ever download or purchase has way too much material for your group to cover. Way too much. And that's on purpose.

Those of us who produce and publish Bible studies have to think broadly. We are trying to include as much good material in each study as we can, because we don't know which specific elements will be useful to a given small group. In other words, we are counting on you to use what is helpful for your group—and we are counting on you to discard the rest.

With that in mind, here are a few guidelines for cutting different types of material within an existing study.

- *Cutting big sections.* Don't feel shy about cutting away entire sections of a Bible study. If the curriculum you are using contains four teaching points and only two of them apply to the "big idea" you have chosen—be ruthless. Cut the study in half and focus on the material that fits smoothly with your "big idea."

  You can also use the knowledge and experience of your group members as a way to filter out unnecessary material. For example, say one of the teaching points in your study is designed to explain the meaning of sanctification, but you know that your group members are already familiar with that doctrine. Feel free to skip that section, or to ask a quick review question and then move on. (The same is true if some of the material in the study conflicts with the beliefs of your group or church.)

- *Cutting discussion questions.* First, make sure to cut out any discussion-killing questions you find in a prewritten study. One of the most common mistakes I see small group leaders make is to try to get through all of the discussion questions included in a Bible study. As in, the group is halfway over and they've only addressed a quarter of the questions, so they try to hurry people along in the name of "keeping things moving."

  That's a big mistake, because few things shut down the activity of the Holy Spirit more efficiently than a group leader scurrying to get everything done. Plus, it makes for lousy conversation and keeps discussion at the surface. The best way to combat this bad habit is to go through the discussion questions before your group meeting and cross out the ones you don't think have much application to your people. Just cross them out. This will help you focus on the questions that are most pertinent to your group. (And if you get through all of those questions, you can always go back and use the ones you crossed out.)

- *Cutting activities.* Many prewritten Bible studies don't include icebreakers or additional activities for worship, prayer and application. So if you come across a study containing that kind of material, count yourself lucky. At the same time, don't feel like you have to use canned activities if they are generic, or if they don't fit what you want to accomplish in a group meeting. You may need to think of something new, and that's okay.

- *A note about participants' guides.* Your curriculum may have included journals or guides or workbooks for the other participants in your small group. If so, don't worry about trying to fill everyone in about the material you've cut out or the changes you've made. Just give clear directions as you guide everyone during the small group meeting. ("We're going to start with an activity that is not in your workbook," or "Let's skip down to question five.")

Here's one more piece of advice on this subject: Be ruthless when you preview and prepare your material each week. You may be cutting out good material. You may be cutting out interesting and useful material. But that's okay, because your goal is to include the best material.

Adding Material (If Necessary)

Once you've cut everything that doesn't connect with your plans for a group meeting, take an objective look at whatever is left over. Is there enough material remaining to cover what you want to accomplish?

Here are a couple time factors to keep in mind as you make that decision:

- For an hour of group discussion, you'll need 5-10 quality discussion questions.

- Icebreakers and learning activities typically last 2-10 minutes.

- A group worship experience will require 15-30 minutes.

- I recommend setting aside 15-30 minutes from each group meeting in order to have a quality prayer experience.

- I also recommend providing at least 15 minutes of hangout time for each group meeting. (This can happen before or after the official group schedule if time is tight.)

There's another set of questions you need to ask before putting the final stamp of approval on a prewritten Bible study. Is the material diverse enough to provide a well-rounded experience? Will it address different learning styles? Will the discussion questions help people engage on at least a few levels? Will you have an opportunity to discuss or practice application?

If you answer no to any of these questions, or if you don't have enough material, then you will need to do some extra work in order to prepare a full-bodied group meeting. This doesn't have to be overly complicated or strenuous. Use the strategies from chapters four to seven to add whatever material you need—just like you were writing an activity or some discussion questions from scratch—and then move on.

Finalizing Your Own Curriculum

There are lots of reasons why small group leaders choose to write their own curriculum. Some do it as a way to save money. Others do it out of necessity when they can't find the right material. And still others do it simply because they enjoy the process.

Whatever reason applies to you, it's important that you make a commitment to a high level of quality. Because writing your own curriculum won't benefit your group if you don't know what you're doing or if you choose to cut corners. That's why the preceding chapters in this section provide detailed instructions for planning the different activities within a small group meeting—things like icebreakers, learning activities, discussion questions, worship, prayer and a "big idea" that keeps everything in focus.

The final step in the process is to organize everything into a plan that can be easily followed once the group meeting gets rolling. And this needs to be a plan that fits how you prefer to operate as a leader.

For example, I am a reading/writing learner who prefers to organize information through words and lists. So, when I put together an agenda for a small group meeting, I usually create an outline.

The following plan is what I developed for the group meeting on James 3:1-12 (including a few notes in brackets):

SCRIPTURE: JAMES 3:1-12

"**Big Idea**": The words we speak can accomplish powerful things both for good and evil. [I've found that writing out the "big idea" in this way helps me keep things focused.]

Icebreaker: Powerful words. [When I think of an icebreaker or learning activity, I usually don't write the whole experience out word for word. But I do jot down several notes to myself so that I'll remember what to do.]

- Bring several newspapers and magazines. Bring scissors, construction paper and glue for a collage.
- Have group members hunt for powerful words (5 minutes).
- Let people share what they found.

- Cut out and glue to make a collage.

Unpacking questions:
- Which words found by other group members did you find to be especially powerful? Why?
- From what source do you most often encounter powerful words?
- When was the last time you wrote or spoke words that you considered to be powerful?

Read James 3:1-12 out loud.

Discussion questions:
- What did you find surprising or significant or confusing about these verses?
- What are the primary images James uses in this passage, and how do you react to them?
- As you are comfortable, talk about moments from your past that support James's claim in verse 8: "[The tongue] is a restless evil, full of deadly poison."
- In what ways can the tongue be used for good?
- In which of these verses (if any) do you believe James is speaking hyperbolically?
- How much control can a human being gain over his or her tongue this side of eternity?
- How do you interpret James's use of rhetorical questions in verses 11-12?
- What steps can we take to minimize the damage caused by the tongue within this small group? (application)

Worship: Collective reading of Psalm 145. (Does anyone want to respond?)

Prayer: Opportunity to confess sin as it relates to our speech.

Again, this is the method of organization I find most efficient and helpful when I prepare for a small group meeting. But you may not be interested in creating an outline, and that's okay.

If you're more of a visual person, you might get better results from arranging the material into boxes or some kind of chart. If you have an auditory learning style, you may want to spend more time talking the lesson plan through with a friend and just jot down a few basic notes.

The point is this: find a system that works for you during your preparation time and during the actual small group meeting.

Beware the Dangers of Unintended Curriculum

Before closing this section on preparing for a small group meeting, I need to address a hidden danger that afflicts many small groups: unintended curriculum.

My wife and I were visiting Southern California on vacation when we decided to stop by Mission San Juan Capistrano—an adobe chapel complex founded by Franciscan monks in 1776. In the back of the mission was a small replica of the gardens that produced much of the monks' food for hundreds of years.

As we walked through the garden, I noticed a particularly leafy bush that had several green lizards lounging among the branches. There was a large sign in front of the bush that read: "Please don't chase or catch our lizards. They lose their tails if you grab them."

Well, you can probably guess the first thought that went through my mind. *I would like to see a lizard's tail fall off.* If I hadn't been with my wife and young (impressionable) son, I'm sure I would have reached out and grabbed a lizard just to see what would happen next.

Thus the danger of unintended curriculum. When we prepare to lead a Bible study as small group leaders, we generally approach each meeting with a certain goal in mind. We have specific principles we would like to explore with our group members—certain truths we hope they understand better after our lesson. That is our intended curriculum. It's what we've outlined in the "big idea." It's what we want to communicate.

For example, consider a small group leader who has structured a discussion around John 3:16: "For God so loved the world that he gave his one and only Son, that whoever believes in him shall not perish but have eternal life." Her intended curriculum would likely include the biblical principles of atonement and redemption.

However, if that leader were to continually stress the idea that Christians "shall not perish but have eternal life" without providing a context or explanation for that terminology, it's possible that a new Christian in the group could come away with the idea that Christians do not experience physical death.

That would be an example of unintended curriculum.

This situation describes the most common form of unintended curriculum—a false belief that is transferred through ignorance about a particular text, or ignorance about proper methods for leading a discussion. In other words, unintended curriculum can pop up if a group leader does a poor job of either interpreting or communicating a passage of Scripture.

But there are other forms of unintended curriculum, including the following:

- *Environment.* The physical or emotional environment of a small group meeting can itself become a kind of curriculum. If group members sit in two rows facing the leader, for example, whatever that leader says will come with an air of authority. When the group sits in a circle, the environment is based more on equality of thought.

- *Priorities.* What we continually emphasize as small group leaders says a lot about what we consider valuable—and not valuable. Therefore, our choice of topics can be an influential source of unintended curriculum. For example, consider a youth leader who spends forty weeks out of a year discussing sexual purity, but only four weeks discussing salvation. He could very easily send a message that God is more interested in restricting our behavior than developing a personal relationship with us.

• *Personal bias.* In a similar way, a leader's opinions on specific subjects can produce unintended curriculum. Think of a group leader railing against the evils of Darwinian evolution. If she chooses to attack the scientists and scientific principles in support of evolution, she can easily impress her group members with the idea that all science is inherently at war with the Bible.

Much of the unintended curriculum that is covertly dished out in small groups is relatively harmless. Theological misinterpretations can be easily corrected by asking questions. Personal biases are regularly overcome through exposure to a variety of opinions and other sources.

But sometimes, unintended curriculum can have deadly and devastating consequences. This happens when a small group leader (or a group member) unintentionally communicates something false about the nature of Christianity itself.

Boredom is probably the most common example. Put simply, when a group leader turns the truths of God's Word into a series of boring questions or activities, he does more than passively fail to deliver his intended curriculum. He actively teaches the group that the Bible itself is boring. And after continued exposure to such unintended curriculum, the members of that group may conclude that the experience of Christianity as a whole is also boring and thus not worth pursuing.

The same is true when we fail to help others see how biblical truths can be applied to everyday life. Or when our personal lives and decisions directly contradict what we have taught or communicated in the group. Or when the tenor of a group discussion is caustic and offensive.

Unintended curriculum can also pop up in the ways we handle the personal dynamics of our small groups. As an example, think back to the most annoying person you've ever experienced in a small group meeting. Now figure out what was the most annoying or disruptive behavior that this person indulged in. Maybe he tried to answer every question and always talked way too much. Maybe she was very judgmental and routinely put down other members of the group. Maybe he fell asleep all the time.

Whatever the behavior was, the response of the group leader (and the group as a whole) taught something to that individual— and to the rest of the group. If the behavior was ignored or left unaddressed, it implied that the negative behavior was acceptable. And chances are that the behavior continued until the group either learned to live with it, disbanded or eventually asked the person to leave. This obviously was not the intention of the leader or the group—it was unintended curriculum.

What you can do about it. My goal in pointing out the nature and reality of unintended curriculum is not to make you paranoid as a small group leader. I don't think it would be profitable for all of us to spend hours examining and reexamining our discussion questions and learning activities in search of any train of thought that could potentially be boring or offensive.

But I would like group leaders to take a step back every now and then and try to examine the small groups we lead from the perspective of those who experience them. Better yet, I would like us to solicit feedback from our group members. What sticks out to them during group meetings? What have they learned in recent weeks? What did they like? What did they dislike? Were they offended by anything that was said? Were they excited?

Taking the time to evaluate ourselves and the experience of our groups will do wonders to make sure that people are learning what we intend to teach them—and nothing more.

PART THREE

Hitting the Trail

Back when I used to play football, my week of athletics was divided into two types of events: practice and the game.

Interestingly, the activities I participated in were similar for both events. I spent most of my time in practices and games running around, pushing other large men, running some more, tackling smaller men and so on. But my frame of mind was drastically different from one to the other. Playing in a game carried a much higher level of intensity—and much greater consequences if I made a mistake.

I feel the same way about the difference between preparing for the activities in a small group meeting and actually leading other people through those activities. Preparation and execution are both important factors in creating an atmosphere that is conducive to spiritual growth. But everything seems more significant when other people are around.

I've written part three of this book to help small group leaders feel more confident and equipped to handle the intensity of a small group meeting:

- Chapter nine provides direction for leading the discussion portion of a group meeting.

- Chapter ten outlines tips and strategies for leading other elements—including fellowship, learning activities, prayer, worship and more.

- Chapter eleven is a troubleshooting guide for some of the common problems that surface during group meetings.
- Chapter twelve explores application on a deeper level and offers inspiration for your important role as a small group leader.

9

The Art of Leading a Small Group Discussion

Do you think it's easy or hard to learn how to drive?

I like to put myself in the shoes of a fifteen-year-old boy when I think about this question. On the one hand, the act of driving itself seems pretty easy. The kid has watched his parents do it for as long as he's been alive, after all, and it must seem to him like the whole experience involves nothing more than pushing a pedal and turning a wheel.

And yet imagine that kid's surprise when someone shows him that thick packet of information people are supposed to study before they take the written test for a driver's license. Or the first time he tries to parallel park. Or the first time he approaches a four-way stop sign without anyone in the car to remind him who has the right of way.

Our fictional kid learns pretty quickly that becoming proficient in the skill of driving won't happen until he achieves mastery over several subsets of abilities, attitudes and rules.

I think leading a small group discussion for the first time is a similar experience. Like driving, the basic idea of leading a discussion is pretty simple: the group leader asks a question, waits for a few people to answer and then asks another question. Repeat until the allotted forty-five minutes are over. Right?

But those of us who have led small group discussions for years understand that so much more is involved. There are skills that need to be learned, habits that need to be formed, principles that need to be applied and more.

And that's the focus of this chapter.

Context: Laying the Groundwork

I mentioned at the beginning of this book that many small group leaders feel the need to teach their group members by providing a lot of information, principles and theories instead of leading an actual discussion. In case there is any ambiguity, let me be clear: this is a bad idea. It's called lecturing, and it should be reserved for professors behind their lecterns (and to some extent pastors behind their pulpits).

But that doesn't mean small group leaders should have nothing to say. We should. In fact, I believe it's important that group leaders spend a little bit of time explaining the context of a Bible passage or topic before the group digs into a discussion.

I also believe that group leaders need to address context on two levels: textual and personal.

Textual context. The textual context of a passage in the Bible is the frame that surrounds that passage and gives it meaning. This frame is made up of several elements:

1. The verses that come immediately before and immediately after the Scripture passage under discussion.

2. The book of the Bible that contains the passage under discussion.

3. All passages of Scripture that were written by the author of the passage under discussion.

4. The Bible as a whole.

5. The cultural and historical setting experienced by the author as he wrote the passage under discussion.

The first two elements listed are often referred to as the "immediate context." They operate like the white lines on both sides of a road—they show us where the text has come from and where it is going, and they provide a boundary that keeps us from wandering away from the text's proper meaning. The final three elements are often referred to as the "broad context." They operate like a map, showing us the country surrounding that particular road on all sides.

Here's my point: One of your jobs as a small group leader is to provide a brief overview of the textual context for the verses your group will be interacting with during a discussion. And you want to provide that overview before the discussion gets started.

You don't want to get carried away, of course. You don't have to dig through a myriad of commentaries and hit your group members with every piece of relevant information you uncover. That would be lecturing, and lecturing is bad.

No, your goal is simply to highlight a few facts and ideas that would not be considered "common knowledge," and that you believe will be helpful to your group members during the discussion. Hopefully that kind of information will be included with the curriculum your group is using. If not (or if you wrote your own material), you should be able to compile some useful information during the process of identifying a "big idea," writing discussion questions and so on.

Personal context. Personal context refers to the experiences and attitudes of your small group members that frame their interaction with each passage of Scripture. In other words, just as the verses before and after a passage of Scripture have an impact on its meaning, the personal stories of your group members will impact how they interact with that passage of Scripture and its meaning. This includes their stories as individuals as well as the collective story of the group as a whole.

To continue the analogy I started earlier, if the broad context of a Scripture passage is like a map, and the immediate context is a single road on that map, then the personal context is the condition of the person attempting to follow that road on that map.

That being the case, another of your jobs as a small group leader is to maintain some level of awareness regarding the condition of your small group members as they prepare to discuss a passage of Scripture. If most of your group seems exhausted, for example, and you had planned on delving into a deep doctrinal exploration of Romans 5, you may need to change things up a bit. Or if you were going to lead a discussion on a Scripture passage that deals with grief (Psalm 22, for example) and you learn that one of your group members has just experienced a death in his or her extended family, you would have a responsibility to include that person's experience in the group's discussion of the text.

The bottom line is this: It is important for you as a leader to highlight the textual context of a Scripture passage in order to help your group explore that passage more fully. In the same way, it is important for you as a leader to point out anything from the lives of your people that may serve as an obstacle or an enhancement to the group's discussion.

An example. My small group recently worked through the book of Revelation, and we started off by exploring the letters to the seven churches in Revelation 2–3. Here are the nuggets of textual and personal context I provided for the group when we studied the letter to the church in Pergamum (Revelation 2:12-17):

- Reminder: all seven letters to the churches follow the same structure. They start with an image of Jesus; they talk about what the church has done well; they talk about what the church has done wrong; they encourage the church to stand strong in the middle of hard times; and they describe a reward for those who do stand strong.

- Pergamum was located on the coast of the country we call Turkey today.

- Pergamum was one of the rare cities in the Roman Empire that was allowed to administer capital punishment, which was called "the right of the sword." This is important for understanding verses 12 and 16.

- I understand that several of you are anxious to start digging into the juicy parts of Revelation that deal with the end of the world and all that. But that starts in chapter four, so we'll need to stay away from those discussions until we get a little farther into the text.

See the idea? Not too long. Not too much information. Just a few helpful facts and observations to prepare the group for an interesting discussion.

How to Facilitate a Group Discussion

It's true that the basic structure of a small group discussion is nothing more than a series of questions and answers between the leader and group members. But in the same vein I could say that playing a guitar is nothing more than moving your hand across the strings, or that Olympic high diving is nothing more than falling into a pool.

In reality, there are several subtle skills and competencies that enable effective discussion leaders to manage the question-and-answer process in a meaningful way. Most group leaders learn these by experience—especially by making mistakes. I have listed some of the more important strategies to help you maximize the former and avoid the latter.

Why silence is your friend. The majority of small group leaders I have encountered are uncomfortable with silence in their groups. They don't like it. They find it awkward and off-putting.

And that's a natural reaction. We live in a noisy world, after all. Between televisions, cell phones, radios and the Internet, something is always pumping sound in our direction—which means a moment of silence during a discussion time is viewed as problematic.

Even more, group leaders often feel like they've made a mistake when they ask a question and receive only an extended period of silence in return. They think the question must have been bad or at least presented in a bad way. As a result, they develop a habit of responding to silence by answering the question themselves or moving on to something else.

Unfortunately, this habit is a deadly enemy of meaningful small group discussion.

That's because silence during a group discussion is almost always a good thing—especially silence that occurs in response to a question. It means your group members are thinking. It means they are processing the question that was asked, comparing it to their understanding of the Scripture passage, integrating that with their own experiences and deciding whether the result is something they want to share with the rest of the group—and all of this takes time.

In fact, it's common for people to spend thirty to sixty seconds processing a complicated question and deciding on a response. That may seem like an eternity to you as a group leader. (Go ahead and have a minute of silence right now to find out.) But that's because you've already been preparing for and thinking about the question for a significant amount of time. You already know what your answer would be.

Your group members, on the other hand, haven't been thinking about the question, which means they will need time to do so during the group—which means you are going to encounter silence. So get used to it.

When a question bombs. Having said all of this, there will be times when you do ask a bad question or present a question in a bad way. There will be times when your group members are silent not because they are thinking but because they have no idea how to respond to what you just said.

You'll know when you've encountered one of these situations because the thirty to sixty seconds will go by without anyone offering even a peep. You'll look at your group members and see them glancing questioningly back and forth at each other. Maybe a couple people will raise their eyebrows or shrug their shoulders or frown in a mystified way. The point is that the body language of your group members will provide more than enough clues to help you decide if they are thinking deeply or are deeply confused.

When you decide that a question has bombed, you have two options:

1. *Rephrase and try again.* If you can think of a way to restate the question, go for it. Try to find a different way to ask the question, or try to approach the topic from a whole new angle.

2. *Let it go and move on.* If you rephrase the question and another thirty to sixty seconds go by without any clarification on the part of your group members, don't press the issue. Say something like, "I guess that's a question we can explore later," and then move on to something else.

One final tip: In most cases, you should resist the urge to answer your own question if nobody else in the group has responded. Also resist the urge to try and rephrase the question in a way that makes your intended answer obvious. The last thing you want to do is give your group members the impression that you are trying to herd them toward a specific idea—and they are too dumb to follow.

Three Important Words Every
Group Leader Should Know

One of the perilous things about serving as a small group leader is that your group members will invariably look to you as an authority on every issue covered during a discussion. Whether you are qualified or not, you will be seen as an expert on the Bible, theology, culture, human interaction and everything in between. This is because you carry the title "leader" and everyone knows it.

That being the case, group members will typically look in your direction if something needs to be decided. When a question pops up about an obscure doctrine, you will be expected to know the answer. When somebody doesn't understand a concept or term, you will be asked to explain. When an argument or controversy develops, you will be asked to figure out who is right and who is wrong.

These situations are common in every small group. They happen to every small group leader. Consequently, most group leaders quickly feel a great deal of pressure to perform. They feel like they should rise to the occasion and become the expert everyone expects—even if they are not qualified.

There are two reasons why you need to resist this temptation at all costs. First, if you "wing it" and provide some kind of expert opinion on an issue you aren't really sure about, there's a good chance you will cause damage. This can range from confusing your group members to false teaching to hurt feelings—all bad things.

Second, when you step into the role of expert and give your opinion about an issue, it usually puts the brakes on any kind of meaningful discussion that might have developed around that issue. Because when the group accepts your words as authoritative, there is nothing left to talk about. This isn't always a terrible thing, but it does have the potential to squelch a lot of positive interaction between your group members, the text and the Holy Spirit.

So, when you don't feel confident about stepping into the role of expert, just use these three simple words: *I don't know.* Be honest and allow the group to continue its exploration as a group. If the group continues to spin its wheels around a question or topic without getting anywhere, you can add three more words: *I'll find out.* This allows the group to move toward something new and gives you a chance to research and find an appropriate answer that can be shared the next time the group gets together.

But what about the times when you do feel confident about sharing your opinion? What about those moments when you want to be the authority in order to answer a question or settle a dispute?

You have two options:

1. *Speak.* Being the group leader doesn't mean you never get to share your opinion or interact with the discussion. You're part of the group, you're part of the discussion, and if you have something to contribute—go for it. Just be aware that your contribution may end that particular branch of the discussion. So use discretion.

2. *Deflect.* If you are worried about becoming the "final answer," you always have the option of deflecting the discussion away from yourself and back to another member (or to the group as a whole). You can say, "I kind of wanted to hear what Mike thinks about this topic," or "I'll share what I think in a minute, but I'd like to get some other opinions on the table first."

Kill the Wabbits

Tangential conversations—also known as "rabbit trails"—are another enemy of meaningful discussion. Of course, rabbit trails don't prevent people from talking or sharing their ideas. Rather, they whittle away the potential for spiritual impact as group members focus their attention on topics that aren't relevant to the discussion.

Again, every small group experiences rabbit trails. They are a natural byproduct of human interaction and conversation. But it's your job as a small group leader to prevent your people from being distracted or harmed by them. And, as in many things, the best way to accomplish this is to simply be honest about your observations. Say something like: "I feel like we're getting off on a tangent here. Can we finish this conversation after the group meeting?"

You're not being mean when you do this. You're not being authoritarian or acting like an ogre. You're doing your job as a spiritual safari guide to keep your group members on the right path.

Maybe you're wondering, *How will I know if my group is wandering down a rabbit trail?* The answer is simple: your "big idea." If the discussion starts moving away from the overarching theme you identified for that particular group meeting, you know it's time to pull everyone back.

I'll address the looming shadow of personality issues in chapter eleven, but I want to take some time now to tackle two common problems that relate specifically to discussion in a small group meeting. I'm referring, of course, to people who talk too much or too little.

When Group Members Talk Too Much

It's a common refrain in the world of small groups today that few barriers can subvert the depth and transforming power of a small group discussion faster than one or more group members who dominate the conversation. And it's certainly true that some people can monopolize entire gatherings with their problems and perspectives, even to the point where they hinder the participation of everyone else in the group.

But I think some of us may need to calm down a bit on the issue of overtalkers in our small groups.

Proceed with caution. Please be aware that some people naturally talk more than others. And that's not necessarily a bad thing. So proceed with caution.

For example, people with an auditory learning style usually process information by speaking out loud. It's just part of how they learn and how they remember facts or ideas they consider to be important. The same is often true of extroverts and social learners.

So, before you label a group member as someone who talks too much, take a step back and try to look objectively at the situation. Are they really being disruptive and controlling, or do they just talk more than you would? Are they negatively affecting the group, or are you just annoyed as an individual?

In other words: Is there really a problem? If your objective answer to that question is no, then you need to let it go. If your answer is yes, then by all means explore the following tips for handling small group members who dominate a discussion.

Be assertive. If you do encounter a genuinely dominating personality, the best solution is assertiveness on the part of the group leader. Specifically:

- *Be assertive before the discussion.* If overtalking is a problem for your group, mention it in a broad way before you start a discussion. Tell the group that you are looking for brief answers and thoughts. You may even consider setting a cap on the amount of time people are allowed to speak on each question—no more than one minute, for example. Also make it known that you want to hear from as many people as possible on each subject.

- *Be assertive during the discussion.* If a group member ignores your request for brevity and begins to monopolize the conversation, the best thing to do is nip it in the bud—even if that means interrupting. Thank the person for his or her contribution, and then move the discussion in another direction by calling on another member or by asking a new question.

- *Be assertive after the discussion.* If a person continually monopolizes the group's time, you may need to talk with that person about it in private. State that you appreciate his or her willingness to contribute to the group's discussions; acknowledge and applaud the depth of his or her answers and opinions. But also be honest in sharing that the frequency and thoroughness of the person's responses can make it difficult for other group members to participate.

  During these conversations it's possible to ask the dominant person for help in encouraging the rest of the group to talk, thus turning a difficult person into an ally.

Manage eye contact. Dominant personalities often associate eye contact from the discussion leader as a green light to talk. They may even interpret it as a request from you to share what's on their mind. Therefore, minimizing eye contact is an effective method for handling group members who talk too much.

To accomplish this without offending the person, invite him or her to sit next to you before the discussion begins. This will decrease the number of times you make direct eye contact with the person, which should also decrease his or her need to talk.

Manage the group's silence. I mentioned earlier that many small group leaders are uncomfortable with silence. Well, that can apply to group members, as well. Sometimes members who feel awkward in times of silence will jump in and answer every question in an effort to end their discomfort. Therefore, by helping them get used to silence as a normal part of group life, you may decrease their need to talk over time.

One way to accomplish this is to ask group members to wait a specific amount of time before responding to a question. Say something like: "People need different amounts of time to process a discussion question and organize their thoughts for a response. To make sure that everyone gets a chance to fully engage with our discussion, I'd like everyone to wait twenty seconds after I ask a question before jumping in."

Of course, it's still possible that dominant group members will be the first people to speak once the time period has expired. If that's the case, talk with them privately using the steps previously outlined, and ask them to wait twenty-five or thirty seconds before speaking in order to make room for others to enter the conversation.

When Group Members Don't Talk Enough

At the opposite end of the spectrum from overtalkers are those group members who almost never say anything during a discussion. These folks can be especially unnerving to small group leaders because they make us feel like we are not doing a good job of leading the discussion.

But again, we as small group leaders need to proceed with caution.

Before you implement any of the following tips, take a time out. Think objectively about the person in question and ask yourself, *Is this really a problem? Is this person refusing to participate in the group, or does he or she just naturally talk less than others?*

If you still believe a problem exists, there are several practical methods you can use to help shy or quiet small group members open up and get involved.

Give them time. First, make sure everyone has enough time to think. Silence is a friend, not an enemy. And if you aren't allowing all of your group members enough time to adequately process a question and come up with a response, they won't be able to contribute.

In other words, be sure their silence isn't your own fault.

Make eye contact. If a group member isn't contributing to the discussion, look directly at him or her as you ask the next question.

Also be aware of the message being sent by your body language. Lean forward and smile as you ask the question. This reassures the person that you are interested in what he or she has to say.

If you are in a group where one or more people have a history of not participating in the discussion, use your choice of seating as an advantage. By sitting directly across from a quiet person, you maximize the amount of eye contact he or she will receive.

Be assertive. Many discussion leaders are hesitant to call on a specific group member for fear of intimidating or embarrassing him or her. But this can be a useful tool for group discussions where it's important that each person participate. Asking for a specific person to respond doesn't need to be authoritative or mean. Instead of demanding an answer, simply ask, "Steve, did you have anything to add?" or "Jamie, did anything strike you as especially interesting?"

When taking this route, be sure to accept "I don't know" as an appropriate answer. Sometimes people genuinely don't have anything they want to add, or what they did plan on saying was mentioned by somebody else. As a discussion leader it's not your role to drag information from each member of the group. Rather, it's your job to politely and assertively let each person know that their opinions are valued and welcomed.

Praise, praise, praise. When a traditionally quiet person does speak out in the middle of a discussion, make sure it becomes a positive experience. Credit the person for the thoughts expressed and be assertive in inviting more by saying something like, "That's a great insight, Pat. We need to hear more from you in the future."

Again, watch your body language and be sure to smile. If a quiet person says something that you don't agree with or that doesn't quite match the topic at hand, don't grimace or smirk. Instead, credit that person for speaking out, then seek out the opinion of another group member who can steer the conversation back on track.

10

Leading a Well-Rounded Group Meeting

I am very fond of well-made Italian cold-cut submarine sandwiches.

In fact, if my diet was completely up to me, I would probably eat Italian cold-cut subs for every meal—maybe with a glass of grape juice on the side. That way I'd be covered for each of the major food groups: grains, fruits, vegetables, meat, dairy and mayonnaise.

Fortunately, my wife buys our food and makes the major decisions regarding what our family eats. And that's why my body enjoys a healthy variety of fuels and is able to function properly (most of the time).

Some group leaders feel the same way about discussion as I feel about Italian cold-cut subs, which means their small group meetings are unbalanced. But no matter how good or productive a group discussion may be, you need to add some variety to your gatherings—or else your group will become spiritually malnourished over time.

That variety includes the other key activities mentioned throughout the course of this book: social interaction, connecting with

God's Word, learning activities, worship and prayer. (It includes application, as well, but that is the subject of chapter twelve.)

This chapter will provide tips and strategies to help group leaders maximize those activities during a small group meeting.

Social Interaction

I mentioned in chapter one that small group leaders cannot force people to grow spiritually. (That job belongs to the Holy Spirit.) It's also true that group leaders cannot force people to connect relationally or enjoy each other's company.

What group leaders can do is set up an atmosphere that is conducive to positive social interaction. In other words, you can provide people with a place to hang out and build relationships without a lot of distractions.

Here are some tips for doing just that:

- *If you have access to a thermostat, set the temperature at sixty-seven degrees.* That may sound cold to you, but trust me—things will warm up plenty when everybody gathers together. Of course, if people are uncomfortable as the group meeting progresses, you can always make adjustments.

- *Use lamps, if possible.* Lamplight is easier on the eyes than overhead fluorescents, and it creates a visually warm and inviting atmosphere.

- *Greet people as they arrive.* Many people have a hard time injecting themselves into a conversation, and they will remain on the sidelines for quite a while if nobody invites them to join in. The best thing you can do is make that invitation as soon as they walk in the door. "Mike and Katie, good to see you! We were just talking about the big picnic next week . . ."

- *Make sure there are enough seats for everyone.* "We're glad you're here" and "There's a spot on the floor" are two statements that don't mesh.

- *Try to have participants sit on the same level.* Many people don't like looking up or down in order to make eye contact and conversation with others. So, to the best of your ability, see if you can have everyone sit at the same eye level; that is, try not to have some people sitting on chairs, others on the floor and others standing up.

- *Have food and drink available.* Everyone likes a snack and a cup of something nice to drink. And those items help in creating a pleasant atmosphere. That doesn't mean you have to buy or prepare them every time, though.[15]

Once you've done what you can to set the stage for a relationally healthy atmosphere, your only other job is to jump in and enjoy some time with your group members.

Working with Teachable Moments

Every small group that gathers together for more than a few months will eventually establish some kind of routine—a rhythm of "doing life together." This is true on a macrolevel as group members see each other during meetings, see each other at church, meet together socially, interact online and so on. This is also true on a microlevel as the group establishes a regular pattern for its group meetings. Telling stories from the past week, discussing the Bible, eating food, sharing prayer requests—all of these are shapes within that pattern.

There's nothing wrong with any of this. It's natural. Your group members learn about one another as a byproduct of these routines, and relationships become more solid. Your group members regularly encounter God's Word in the midst of these routines, and they grow both intellectually and spiritually.

The frustrating thing for us as group leaders is that these advances come slowly. They happen gradually, for the most part, and they happen below the surface. That means we don't always see a lot of fruit in the lives of our group members—we don't get many tangible signs that we are doing a good job leading our people into life-changing encounters with each other and the Holy Spirit.

There are other times, however, when something happens in the group that breaks everyone free from these regular patterns—moments that pull the group away from its routine and into something different.

It is in these moments that group members often experience a jump of some kind. Relationships solidify quickly into a deeper bond. Something clicks in a person's mind that enables him or her to truly understand and apply a doctrinal truth. Someone experiences conviction about an area of sin and confesses it openly.

I refer to these times as "teachable moments."

Keep your eyes open. It's hard to write authoritatively about teachable moments because they are so difficult to pin down. They are spontaneous, unplanned bursts of insight or a sudden movement of the Holy Spirit.

Still, teachable moments do tend to fall into these broader categories:

- *Conflict.* People are sinful, and when you gather them together enough times, there will eventually be a clash. This will happen in your small group, but it's not something you need to be afraid of. When handled correctly (see chap. 11), conflict motivates people to speak truthfully and open up about their feelings and experiences. Indeed, a brief burst of conflict is often the spark that ignites a deep friendship.

- *Moments of extraordinary fun.* Conflict is not the only thing that solidifies relationships. When group members have a chance to really enjoy each others' company—a camping trip, a shared hobby, an extended conversation—surprisingly powerful bonds can form.

- *Conviction of sin.* Another area directed by the Holy Spirit is conviction of sin. Sometimes people feel convicted while discussing a Scripture passage, other times it happens while they verbalize a prayer request—and other times it happens in a completely unexpected situation. But the end result is usually the same for the person experiencing conviction: an impulse to confess their sin and commit to repentance.

  Of course, people don't always respond to this kind of conviction. Many people fight it or hold off on taking action until they can speak with someone privately. Others don't respond verbally but show other signs of a deeper moment—things like weeping, becoming unusually withdrawn or becoming confused.

- *Bursts of insight.* As I mentioned earlier, there are times when group members are struck by a new understanding of a doctrine or biblical truth. All the pieces come together and they "get it." They not only understand what God is saying in his Word but how that truth applies to their lives—and how their lives will need to change because of it. Again, this is usually initiated by the Holy Spirit, and group members often respond by sharing what they have learned with the rest of the group.

- *Moments of crisis.* Sometimes group members will open up about a crisis they are experiencing—maybe they lost a job, maybe a loved one is seriously ill, maybe they are in financial peril. Sharing something of this magnitude takes extreme courage and vulnerability, which carries the potential for a powerful moment within the group.

As a small group leader, one of your more important jobs is to keep an eye out for these kinds of teachable moments.

Tips and tricks. Maybe you're wondering, *What am I supposed to do when our group experiences something like that?*

Good question. I generally have two guidelines when it comes
to responding to teachable moments as a small group leader:

1. *Call a halt to the routine.* When something powerful happens in
   your small group, you as the leader must call attention to it. You
   cannot allow a potentially life-changing moment to be ground
   down under the wheels of routine.

   Say something like, "Susan, I'm so thankful you were willing
   to share that with us. If you don't mind, I'd like to take a break
   right now and pray as a group that God will be with you in this
   situation." Or "I know we have a lot of discussion questions to
   get through, but that was an amazing insight, Jim. Can we talk
   about that a little more?" Or even "Okay, I think some of us are
   feeling a little attacked right now. Let's see if we can all take a
   deep breath and start again."

2. *Be ready to get out of the way.* Once you've called the group's attention to a potential teachable moment, it's important that you
   don't try to maintain control over that moment. Teachable moments are not facilitated. They occur and grow organically,
   driven either by the Holy Spirit or the emotions and needs of
   your group members.

If some of this seems a little vague to you, I understand. Teachable
moments are mysterious and profound events, and they defy a lot
of step-by-step analysis. But they are real, and they do have the
potential to make a significant impact in the growth of your small
group—if you are watching and willing to embrace the mystery.

Leading Learning Activities

The bad news about icebreakers and learning activities is that they
take a bit of time to prepare—especially when you first start using
them in a small group. But the good news is that preparing ahead of
time usually helps things run smoothly during the actual meeting.

In fact, your role in leading a learning activity can be summed up in two words: *explain* and *retain.*

If you plan on having group members go around the circle and talk about their favorite Christmas gift as a child, then you won't need to offer much additional explanation. But if you plan on leading a more robust learning activity, you should take an extra minute to make sure that everyone knows what's going on.

Give a detailed explanation of what will happen during the activity, what supplies will be used (if any) and what will be expected of your group members. Ask if anyone has any questions, and don't start the activity until you are reasonably sure that everyone understands the directions and is capable of carrying them out. Also make sure everyone knows that you're available to answer questions during the activity, as well.

Once the activity gets started, your other responsibility is to ensure that things don't get out of control—which is what I mean by *retain.* Sometimes people can drift away from the purpose of an activity when they're having fun and moving around. So keep an eye on things and be ready to rein participants back in if necessary.

Also retain an awareness of how much time has gone by. If you have allotted a specific amount of time for a learning activity, give the group regular reminders about how much time is left. "Okay folks, we'll take two more minutes to finish cutting out newspaper clippings, and then we'll all present what we've found."

Leading Worship

There are several variables involved with leading times of worship in a small group meeting—lots of activities to choose from and lots of ways to adapt those activities based on the makeup of your group. I recommend checking out appendix one at the back of this book to find several resources on SmallGroups.com that cover the topic of worship in greater detail than I have space to offer here. Still, I do want to mention some general guidelines that you may find helpful as you lead your group members in times of worship.

For example, don't be afraid of silence during worship experiences. In fact, I highly recommend using silence as a key tool to enhance your times of worship. People are able to reflect and contemplate more fully in quietness than when they are being directed to do something or say something. That means you can provide a richer experience of worship by using silence in the middle of Communion, before or after a Scripture reading, in between songs, and more.

Speaking of songs, keep the following in mind when you include music in your worship:

- *Have variety in the songs you choose.* Some worship songs are snappy; some are somber. Some people like contemporary music; others like hymns. So, when you pick out a set of songs for a particular group meeting (and I recommend three to five), try to incorporate some variety.

- *Put some thought into the order of the songs.* Another benefit to having a diverse set of songs is that you can match the tone of the activities around your worship time. For example, if you worship after an icebreaker where the group was up and moving around, you should start with one or two peppy songs. Then you can finish with songs that have a slower tone, which will help your group transition to prayer or discussion. The same is true the other way, of course—if you worship after a time of prayer and contemplation, start with a song that is more somber.

- *Provide lyrics.* You probably won't have hymnals or PowerPoint slides in your group meeting, but you should still make an effort to give people the words to the songs you choose. This doesn't have to be complicated—putting the lyrics on one or two sheets of paper is more than acceptable. You could also provide group members with a binder of lyric sheets and have them add new songs to it over the course of the group. (Make sure you obey copyright laws if you do start copying music.)

Here's one more thing to consider: Maybe you shouldn't be leading worship at all. Maybe that role should be fulfilled by someone else within the group. Frankly, leading a small group meeting is a draining experience—especially when you have to be "on" for the entire time. It is an act of offering yourself intellectually and emotionally in order to lead others.

For that reason, identifying one or more group members to take charge of worship can be a blessing in several ways. It provides you with a chance to recharge. It allows the worship leader to become more invested in the group through increased responsibility. And it helps the group experience more than one leadership style.

When you look for a volunteer to help with worship, don't assume it has to be someone who plays an instrument. That's a good place to start, but you should also keep your eyes open for the participants who become most engaged in your group's worship experiences. Do a person's eyes light up when you announce a Scripture reading or moment of contemplation? Does anyone display passion while singing a hymn? Has a group member already started taking the lead during some worship experiences?

If so, you've just identified a potential worship leader for your group.

Leading Prayer

I've read a lot of good material on the intersection of small groups and prayer, but none of it has been more helpful than Andrew Wheeler's book *Together in Prayer*. If you plan on praying during your small group meetings, you need to read this book. Trust me.

Wheeler uses the metaphor of playing an instrument to describe the act of prayer. When we pray privately, we are soloists playing our music for God alone. But when we pray in a group, we are a symphony—a collection of individuals working together to lift a pleasing song toward our heavenly audience.

Unfortunately, the members of a typical small group are usually not very good at working together. As Wheeler notes:

> Often group prayer turns out to be more like a collection of soloists each playing their own piece than a concerted voice arising out of teamwork. One particularly experienced soloist plays a very long piece, and others are intimidated to follow. Multiple soloists each play a piece of their own, but there is no relationship between the pieces, no common refrain. The result is a cacophony of individual prayers and not true community prayer—not the picture Jesus had in mind in Matthew 18:19-20 when he spoke of two or more people coming together and agreeing in prayer.[16]

Does that sound like your small group? If so, I'm afraid the problem boils down to a lack of leadership. People need to be taught how to work together in prayer—it doesn't come naturally. And as the group leader, you are the one to do the teaching. That's the bad news.

The good news is that you only need to communicate two basic principles in order to begin solving the problem: the two dimensions of group prayer and the role of agreement in group prayer.

The two dimensions of group prayer. Praying as a small group involves two distinct dimensions: the vertical (our connection with God) and the horizontal (our connection with the other members of the group). Dissonance occurs when group members concentrate primarily on one dimension while ignoring the other.

For example, some people focus on the vertical dimension of prayer. They don't pay much attention when others are praying because they are planning out what they will say when it's their turn. When their turn comes, they sometimes deliver long, winding

prayers that ignore the needs or preferences of those around them.
I think most people in small groups are the opposite, though.
They get so caught up with the horizontal dimension that they
fail to establish any kind of connection with God. This happens
when group members feel pressure to sound impressive when
they pray, resulting in a lot of jargon and clichés—or when they
choose to lace their prayers with subtle hints and pieces of advice directed toward the people they are praying for. This is also
reflected when a group member gets annoyed or frustrated by
the way other people choose to pray; he or she is focusing on
what others are doing wrong rather than participating in the
prayer experience.

As a small group leader you need to help your group members
understand these two dimensions of group prayer. Even more,
you need to give them a vision of what prayer can be like when
both dimensions are balanced—when the group is working as a
team to create a single voice of adoration, thanksgiving and supplication to God.

The role of agreement in group prayer. Wheeler refers to this
vision as "praying to God with people." As each person prays out
loud, his or her focus is primarily on God, not on the other group
members. The prayers themselves are humble requests for God to
intervene according to his will.

While one person is praying out loud, the other members of the
group need to do more than passively listen to that person's words.
They need to actively agree with the requests and praises being
lifted up—to focus on supporting the person praying and echoing
his or her words.

This kind of agreement takes different forms for different people. Some prefer to express their support in whispered words—
"Yes, Jesus" or "Please help him, Lord." Others prefer to remain
silent and internally repeat the words being spoken. Still others
focus on visual representations of the requests and praises offered

by other members of the group.

The method of agreeing in prayer is not important, and group members should be encouraged to use whatever techniques come naturally and feel comfortable. What is important is that the people in your group actively engage in prayer even when they are not saying anything out loud.

Practical tips and tricks. Here are some final bits of advice I would like to offer before I close out this section on small group prayer:

1. *Set boundaries for prayer requests.* Maybe your group decides to only mention requests pertaining to people within the group and their immediate families. Maybe you ask group members to list no more than three requests each. Whatever you decide, there need to be a few reasonable boundaries in place to ensure that group members don't feel like they are wasting their time listening to (and praying for) frivolous requests.

2. *Provide pen and paper.* Give your group members an opportunity to write down the requests of others if they so choose. This is beneficial for prayer within the group, but it also gives everyone a chance to continue praying for the requests throughout the week.

3. *Keep a prayer log.* Speaking of keeping track of requests, I highly recommend that your group appoint someone to keep a record of the prayers and praises listed during each group meeting. The goal is twofold: to make sure that requests are continually lifted up before God, and to provide an official record of answered prayers so that the group can get a picture of God's faithfulness over time.

One twist on this idea is to create a Facebook page or some other kind of accessible record for your group and your prayers. This probably should include a password so that private prayers aren't made public.

4. *Encourage different prayer postures.* For some people, kneeling on the ground helps them adopt an attitude of submission and reverence during prayer; for others, kneeling on the ground just

makes their knees hurt. When it's time to pray, encourage your group members to use whatever posture they feel comfortable with. Kneeling, standing, sitting, hands clasped, hands raised— whatever helps your group members connect with God and agree with the others.

11

When Things Don't Go as Planned

I have a weird ritual I go through whenever I purchase a new electronic gadget or gizmo. As soon as everything is put together or installed, I pull out the instruction manual and read the troubleshooting section at the back. Doing so gets me familiar with all of the things that can go wrong, along with the different symptoms, so that I'll know what to watch for if anything starts going haywire.

That's the basic idea behind this chapter.

The difference is that electronic gizmos are mass-produced, while no two small groups are exactly the same. Each group is made up of unique individuals forming relationships and interacting with each other in unique ways. So it's impossible for someone like me to anticipate the specific malfunctions that may pop up in a small group like yours.

Still, there are a number of problems and confusing situations that seem to be universal to the small group setting. Some of them have been addressed in the earlier pages of this book; others are addressed in different places throughout the publishing world, including SmallGroups.com.

The small group malfunctions addressed in this chapter are issues I believe to be serious enough to warrant some expert assistance, yet common enough that there's a good chance you will be dealing with them at some point in your career as a small group leader.

When Group Members Experience Strong Emotions

People are emotional beings. And while most of us prefer to keep most of our emotions in check most of the time, one of the signs of a healthy small group is that participants become more and more comfortable sharing their feelings. It's a natural byproduct of deepening relationships.

That being the case, it's likely that you will encounter a burst of stronger-than-normal emotions at some point in your career as a small group leader. Maybe a group member begins sobbing uncontrollably out of guilt, fear or grief. Maybe someone vents a lot of angry words about a difficult or frustrating situation. Or maybe someone erupts in a shower of joy.

Whatever the case, it's important that you as the leader set the tone for how the group will respond to these strong emotions. Here are a few guidelines to keep in mind as you do so:

- *Listen.* Actively listen to the person expressing a strong emotion. Your first reaction may be to change the subject or find a way to help that person calm down, but you must resist these temptations. Let the person speak and make it clear to the group that you are listening.

- *Affirm.* One of the best things you can do in this situation is name the emotion being expressed. "I hear you expressing a lot of [anger, grief, fear]." Validate the emotion instead of giving the impression that "you shouldn't feel that way."

- *Offer to help.* When the initial venting of emotion subsides and you have been able to affirm what the group member is experiencing, give permission for the group member to seek help. "What can all of us do right now to help?" And make sure you include the entire group instead of attempting to handle everything by yourself. If the emotional member is close with someone else in the group, allow that person to offer comfort or a listening ear as needed.

- *Respond appropriately.* If the group member is embarrassed and asks for a minute to regain control, allow him or her to do so. Offer the use of an empty room and ask if he or she would like to go alone or take a trusted friend. If the group member wants to talk—maybe to confess a sin, maybe to vent, maybe to seek advice—stop what the group was doing and listen.

- *Affirm again.* When the situation has passed and the group member is returning to a more normal state, make sure to affirm his or her willingness to share. "It takes a lot of courage to open up the way you did, and I want to say thank you for trusting all of us with those feelings."

When Your Group Experiences Conflict

Not only are people emotional beings, we are imperfect as well. We're sinful. And when imperfect, sinful, emotional people gather together on a regular basis, they eventually clash.

We have to face it: conflict is an inevitable part of every small group. Including yours.

But not all conflict is the same. In general terms, I like to break small group conflict into two separate types: short-term and long-term.

Short-term conflict. Sometimes conflict erupts spontaneously between group members. It can be the result of a flash-in-the-pan reaction to something that was said, a debate that gets a little overheated or just a group member having a really bad day.

Here are some basic guidelines to help you manage these small group solar flares:

- *Don't ignore these issues.* If you don't like getting in the middle of conflict (and few people do), your first instinct might be to ignore flare-ups between group members. But that's a bad idea. Failing to address a negative behavior sends the message to the rest of the group that such behaviors are acceptable. This is especially true if one or more group members speaks in a way that is rude, offensive, overly sarcastic or mean. Your group will not remain a safe place for people if such behavior is tolerated and overlooked.

  At the same time, you may encounter a situation where your group responds appropriately to conflict or negative behavior without your leadership. And that's more than okay. If your group has reached a place where participants point out negative behavior and address it on their own—your job is that much easier, and you can feel free to remain in the background until needed.

- *Address conflict quickly.* Another bad habit group leaders often fall into is trying to address a flare-up after the group meeting is over. They don't want to embarrass the people involved or make a big deal in front of the whole group, so they wait. But people rarely talk about what happened after a little time has gone by. They bury the negative feelings associated with the incident and tell each other, "It's not a big deal." But those negative feelings don't go away, and they can often transform into long-term dislike.

  It's much better to address a short-term conflict quickly, while the emotions are still close to the surface. This is the best time for people to express themselves, listen to another point of view, and legitimately forgive and move on.

- *Address conflict as a group.* Don't feel like you have to act alone in addressing an outbreak of short-term conflict. If something happened within the public view of your small group, it can be addressed publically by the group. Your job as the leader is to highlight what just happened. "I think this conversation is starting to get a little overheated. Does anyone else agree?" "I feel like what Henry just said was over the line. What does everyone else think?"

- *Use your judgment about moving forward.* One of the hardest things to figure out in these kinds of situations is when they are over. When can the group move on and resume a normal meeting? Since each round of conflict is different, that decision has to be made on a case-by-case basis.

  The only advice I have is to use your best judgment. If everyone involved seems genuinely sorry for the incident and ready to move forward, then it's over. If one or more people are still smoldering or don't accept the gravity of what just happened, you may need to continue the conversation. And if one or more people are becoming more and more upset, you may need to call a time-out and speak with them privately (or have another trusted group member do so).

  If things get to the point where a reasonable solution seems out of the question, you probably need to step in and table the discussion until a later date. Give people a chance to calm down and then address the issue during the next group meeting at the latest. (If you can get the parties together and figure things out before the next meeting, that's even better.)

  Long-term conflict. Whereas short-term conflict is spontaneous, long-term conflict is more sinister and brooding. Sparked by any number of things—unaddressed short-term conflict, differences in personalities, a perceived insult—long-term conflict can bubble below the surface of relationships indefinitely if left unaddressed.

This kind of conflict carries with it the potential to seriously damage a small group—even cause it to break apart. It puts people on eggshells and gradually erodes any feelings of safety and peace initially experienced by the group. For that reason, it needs to be dealt with and resolved in a serious way.

For example, I once had two people in my small group who disliked each other right off the bat. Their personalities clashed, and they were never able to find any common ground. Still, they tried not to make a big deal about it; each person handled the situation by avoiding the other person as much as possible.

After a couple months, it became clear to me that avoidance was not going to be a long-term solution. When one person made a statement during discussion, the other would automatically disagree. Both individuals started speaking sarcastically to and about the other, and soon the group was inflicted with miniature eruptions of anger and unkind speech. Each group meeting was weighed down by a palpable sense of tension.

Unfortunately, I made the mistake of trying to resolve the issue by serving as a bridge between the two rivals. I had several conversations with each person, but always in isolation from each other. I was trying to bring reconciliation by acting like a middleman, and it didn't work. One of the rivals ended up leaving the group, and the other left a few months later.

So, that brings up the question, how should a group leader respond in a situation where two or more group members are experiencing serious long-term conflict?

One option is to involve the leadership of your church or some other kind of outside mediator. The main job of the small group leader in these situations is to talk with each of the people involved and help them see the danger of what is going on and agree to seek a resolution.

Once the rivals are ready to address the problem, there are two ways to go about solving it. First, the rival group members can meet privately with the group leader—and if necessary, with a pastor or mediator. This certainly can be effective and has certain advantages for keeping private matters private when necessary.

But after my failed experience as a middleman, I prefer the second option: inviting the pastor or mediator to the group and resolving the conflict as a whole-group experience. It's more than likely that everyone in the group is aware of the conflict, and finding a public resolution is effective in bringing healing for the entire group.

To make this happen, I like the conflict-resolution method proposed by Mark Bonham, former executive director of Open Hearts Ministry:

1. The group leader should define the conflict as he or she recalls it. "Our conflict is about the differences between Jim's way and Mary's way of engaging the group and the tension that we and they are experiencing as a result."

2. Ask the group members if the conflict has been defined correctly as they recall it. Go around the circle and give each person an opportunity to respond. Some will have something to say; others may simply nod their head in agreement.

3. Ask, "How has this conflict felt to you?" Or "What has been stirred up in you as the conflict has become evident?" The purpose here is to give each group member an opportunity to acknowledge and express his or her feelings. There is no right or wrong answer here. Silence or withholding does not support the conflict resolution process, so encourage everyone to speak.

4. Invite group members to ask questions of any other group member for clarity. Be careful to make sure that one person does not dominate this time or the process will lose momentum for the others.

5. Ask each person, "What were you hoping would happen in this

meeting?" "What did you want for yourself?" "What did you want for Jim, Mary or the group?"

6. Ask each person what needs to happen for them to feel that this is a safe and healthy group again. What a member may express may not necessarily be something the group can guarantee (for example, that the conflict will never happen again). The leader's role is to make sure all have been heard and to stay engaged in the process for the sake of the group. Allowing the process to stall or wander will make the group feel unsafe and lose trust.

7. Ask each person, "Can you recommit to this group?" If someone says no, go back to points three and four and try again. Typically a group will want to get going again and not remain stalled.

Again, this process is something that should only be used when participants have a major problem that is affecting the life of the group. This process relies on the integrity of the group to call one another out. At its best, it is a way for the body of Christ to minister to each other.[17]

How to Handle Theological Disagreements

There's no doubt that the Bible is the most influential and important book in human history. Unfortunately, it is not always the easiest to understand.

That's why theological disagreements and debates are so common among Christians. And yes, theological conflict will pop up regularly in your small group. Usually things stay pretty tame, and these kinds of discussions are often educational on many levels. But sometimes a theological disagreement can become pretty feisty.

I hate to sound like a broken record, but since every person in every group is different, there is no canned method of addressing vigorous theological disputes. But the following approaches have worked for me and many others in the past. It's up to you as the group leader to choose which method is best for each situation.

Take no action. As a mentioned earlier, most theological debates are harmless—even beneficial. They offer a way for group members to broaden their horizons and be exposed to different points of view. They can serve as an "iron sharpens iron" moment.

So before you take any action to reign in or redirect a theological discussion, ask yourself whether anything harmful is going on. If not, relax and join in the discussion.

Use outside authority. You may not have seen it, but the chances are very good that the leaders of your church have put together a statement of beliefs or some other document outlining the doctrinal positions held by the church.

It's important that you get a copy of this document and keep it handy. Then, when a theological debate starts to get a little heated, you can produce it as a source of outside authority. "Here's what our church leaders have written about this particular issue." (Or "Here is the position of our denomination.")

This won't always end the discussion, of course. (Believe it or not, there are people out there who disagree with their church leaders.) But sometimes it will. And sometimes it will provide a break in the conversation that allows you to suggest an alternate method for resolving the issue (including the methods listed below).

Finish it later. If your group has engaged in a theological debate that falls within the boundaries of your "big idea," that's great. You probably won't want to stop it.

But if group members are going back and forth on an issue that is irrelevant to the main focus of the gathering, you are well within your rights as a group leader to ask that they continue the debate at another time. Say something like, "Folks, I know this is an interesting topic, but I think we should talk about it after we have our final prayer a little later. Let's get back to question four on our study guides."

Offer to research and reconvene. Sometimes a theological conversation goes round and round in circles because it suffers from a lack of information. You'll hear participants say things like, "I'm pretty sure I read that somewhere in the Gospel of John" or "Doesn't Paul say something about salvation and works?" But nothing moves forward because people can't get a clear view of the theological terrain.

In these situations, you as the group leader can step in and say, "I don't know about everyone else, but I need some more information before I figure out exactly what I believe on this topic. What if we all do some research this week and talk about our discoveries at the next meeting?"

One warning, though: Don't use this as a way to get out of a discussion in hopes that your group members lose interest in the topic. Some of them will probably forget doing any research, but not all of them. And those who do work to form an opinion will be disappointed if you ignore their efforts at the next meeting.

Address heresy with compassion and truth. There are common beliefs in the Christian faith, and then there are essential doctrines—key principles laid out in Scripture that deal directly with our understanding of God, our condition and salvation. There are denominational differences surrounding what is essential, of course, but a large percentage of Christians can find agreement over most major historical doctrines.

For example, here is the statement of faith written by the National Association of Evangelicals:

- We believe the Bible to be the inspired, the only infallible, authoritative Word of God.

- We believe that there is one God, eternally existent in three persons: Father, Son and Holy Spirit.

- We believe in the deity of our Lord Jesus Christ, in His virgin birth, in His sinless life, in His miracles, in His vicarious and atoning death through His shed blood, in His bodily resurrection, in His ascension to the right hand of the Father, and in His personal return in power and glory.

- We believe that for the salvation of lost and sinful people, regeneration by the Holy Spirit is absolutely essential.

- We believe in the present ministry of the Holy Spirit by whose indwelling the Christian is enabled to live a godly life.

- We believe in the resurrection of both the saved and the lost; they that are saved unto the resurrection of life and they that are lost unto the resurrection of damnation.

- We believe in the spiritual unity of believers in our Lord Jesus Christ.[18]

So, what should you do if a group member expresses a belief or opinion that contradicts one of these essential doctrines? Maybe someone casually mentions that they are going to heaven because they are a good person. Maybe someone asserts that the Father, Son and Holy Spirit are all different beings.

Whatever the case, it's important that your first reaction to their statement be one of compassion and kindness. Judgment and condemnation are inappropriate in any situation, including this one. And be sure to avoid giving the impression that the person should have known better. It's no good correcting a person's intellectual understanding of Christianity if you violate its core principles in the process.

At the same time, notice I did not say you should react in a way that demonstrates acceptance for false beliefs. Nor should you ignore a clear violation of vital doctrine. As a group leader, you have a responsibility to help your people grow, and this is a prime opportunity.

That being the case, I recommend you take the following steps when confronted with heresy:

1. Label the doctrine under discussion. To the best of your ability, highlight the theological issue being challenged by the group member's statement or belief. Also give your impression of the church's position. "I think what we're talking about is the doctrine of the Trinity. The traditional belief is that the Father, Son and Holy Spirit are all the same being, which is why the Bible talks about 'one God.'"

2. Invite affirmation from the rest of the group. One thing you don't want to do is get in a one-on-one discussion with the group member in question. Rather, open things up and allow the entire group to be part of the conversation. This should not be an invitation to gang up on a member of your group. The idea is to ask, "What does everyone else think about this issue?" Not "Who else wants to explain why this person is wrong?"

3. Look to sources of authority. All of the essential doctrines of Christianity have clear support from the pages of Scripture. So, the best opportunity to resolve the issue is for your group to find the passages that relate to the doctrine being discussed. Another option is to seek counsel from your church's statement of beliefs.

4. Follow up as needed. Helping a group member get a better handle on key doctrinal issues is a great opportunity for growth. So don't miss it. Offer to meet the person for coffee later in the week in order to discuss the issues in greater detail. Make a phone call a couple days after the meeting and thank the person for his or her willingness to exchange ideas; ask if he or she has any questions now that some time has passed. You can even offer to connect the group member with one of the pastors from the church.

One more thought about addressing theological and doctrinal disagreements in a small group: it's worth the effort. It's not always fun, and it can sometimes be a real drag on the momentum of a group meeting—especially when the conversation gets heated or you need to address potential heresy.

But it is worth it. I feel strongly about this because I feel strongly that doctrine matters. What we believe matters, because belief is often the first step toward action and life change.

Plus, if your small group is not a place for serious discussion about biblical doctrine, where else can your group members turn? Most churchgoers aren't going to walk up to a pastor on Sunday morning and express doubts or confusion about a particular doctrine; nor are they likely to plow through commentaries for a bit of light reading.

In today's church, small groups are the best place—and sometimes the only place—for laypeople to clarify what they believe and why they believe it. So don't ignore the opportunity.

When a Bible Study Bombs

No matter how well you choose Bible studies or write your own material, there will be some group meetings where everything seems to go wrong. The icebreaker is a dud. The discussion questions are more confusing than stimulating. Even the prayer time seems uncharacteristically dull.

So, how should a group leader react to a clunker of a group meeting?

The best thing to do, in my opinion, is honestly share your evaluation with the group. "Folks, I'm feeling like things are a little off tonight. How are the rest of you feeling about the vibe of the group right now?" If your group members don't share your discomfort, you probably need to just buckle down and continue with the plan.

But if your feelings are echoed by the group, you can all work together to come up with a different approach. Maybe people are tired and everyone just needs to relax and have some fun for an hour. Maybe people would like the opportunity to spend more time in prayer or worship or talking about ways to serve.

Whatever you decide, you shouldn't have any trouble declaring a mulligan and getting back into the swing of things the following week.

But that brings up another situation to consider: what if a curriculum is bombing in a more long-term way? Meaning, everyone was excited about a particular Bible study, you all paid for different copies of the material, and the group has been using it for a few weeks—but things aren't going well. What should you do then?

Again, the best advice I can give you is to honestly share your feelings with the group. And if a majority of your group members are dissatisfied with the experience, there is no shame in abandoning the curriculum. Never be afraid to change something that isn't working, and never push forward with something that is unproductive simply because you don't know what else to do.

When a Group Member Just Doesn't Fit In

If you read much of the prose coming out of the small groups world, it won't be long before you come across the subject of group members who don't fit in. The main buzzwords for these individuals are *difficult people* or *EGRs* (extra grace required).

To be honest, I think a lot of what has been written and produced about this subject is baloney. Or hooey. Or whatever word you prefer to use about a topic that people treat as important when it really is not.

I know I've said this several times already, but it bears repeating: every small group in the world today is made up of human beings. And every human being in the world today is imperfect. We are all sinful. We are all emotional. We are all unpredictable and perplexing and just a bit unstable.

In other words, we are all difficult people. We all require enormous amounts of grace.

That's why I get irritated when I hear things like, "Every group has an EGR person—and if you can't figure out who that person is, it's probably you." Because I don't like the idea of giving a small group leader the power to point a finger at a member of the group and say, "He's the difficult one" or "She's the EGR."

No matter our best intentions, it changes our perception of an individual when we label them in that way. They cease to be an equal member of the group in our eyes—someone to love, serve and enjoy. Instead they become someone to manage, someone to control or someone to avoid.

And that's a shame.

I'll get off my soapbox now. I actually do believe there are times when a truly difficult person joins a small group. And by *difficult* I mean someone with a legitimate psychological or personality disorder.

Some of these individuals have an extreme form of emotional neediness—they dominate entire group meetings by constantly talking about their problems, call people at odd hours or attempt to reach an uncomfortable level of intimacy with members of the group. This can be a temporary state brought on by a crisis, and even when things are more permanent, these individuals can sometimes function well in a caring and patient group.

There are others who are incapable of functioning normally in social situations. They suffer from conditions such as bipolar disorder, autism, addiction and mental illness—something that involves a clinical diagnosis, in other words. It is rare for these individuals to "work" in a typical small group.

Here's the problem with these distinctions: if it's a bad idea to label someone as "extra grace required," I certainly don't want to imply that group leaders should start attempting to diagnose clinical disorders. Rather, if a group member is regularly affecting a group in a negative or harmful way, I recommend the following steps:

- *Get some help.* Unless you are a trained counselor or psychiatrist, you should not attempt to minister to this kind of person on your own. The first thing you should do is consult with a pastor or staff person from your church. Be clear about what you have witnessed from the individual in the group, and don't leave that meeting without a defined plan of action for moving forward.

- *Set boundaries.* If you and your pastor decide the person in question can remain in your group, the next step is to set up a meeting with all three of you. The goal of this meeting is to establish ground rules and boundaries for the challenged person's participation in the group.

    I know that may sound a little harsh, but it can actually be an encouraging step for the difficult person. Most people who have trouble fitting in with a group are not unaware of the situation—especially those with emotional issues or social problems. They can sense that something is wrong, that people are uncomfortable around them, but they usually can't put a finger on the specific causes. So, having a meeting to establish boundaries gives these individuals something to focus on and a goal for improvement.

- *Inform the group.* You can inform the group by holding a group meeting without the difficult person, or by meeting with (or calling) group members one at a time. One purpose of these meetings is to bring group members up to speed on both the difficulty faced by the person in question and the boundaries that have been set in place to help that person become integrated into group life. A second purpose is to rally the group around the potential for genuinely life-changing ministry that this individual represents. They have the chance to represent Christ in a powerful way.

- *The last resort.* Including a truly difficult person in a small group will be difficult. And although the rewards can be substantial—both for the person in question and the other group members—there are times when things simply don't work out. If you as the group leader feel the situation is becoming unbearable for the group, you should again meet with your pastor and talk about removing the person from the group. This should be the last option explored, but it does need to be an option.

If you do ask the individual to leave the group, work with your pastor to present him or her with another option for community involvement. This could include a support group or regular sessions with a pastor or counselor.

12

Application and Inspiration

Here's what the apostle James said in the first chapter of his epistle: "Do not merely listen to the word, and so deceive yourselves. Do what it says" (v. 22).

That's a command directed at individual Christians, for sure. But it's also directed at small groups of individual Christians who regularly gather together for the sake of experiencing God and advancing his kingdom. Because small groups that do not practice application have very little chance of experiencing spiritual transformation.

If we think otherwise, we are deceiving ourselves.

Inward Versus Outward

"Should my small group be open or closed?" That's a common question in the world of small groups, and one that receives different answers from different people. (If you're not familiar with the lingo, "open" groups allow visitors and new members, while "closed" groups do not.)

Open groups are generally viewed more positively because they provide opportunities for connection and growth—in individual groups and an entire ministry. However, there are certainly times when closed groups are appropriate and beneficial. Recovery groups are a good example. It's also becoming more common for groups to remain closed during a particular study or semester, and then open for new members at specific points during the year. (I refer to these groups as "semi-open.")

In many ways, the debate between open and closed groups misses the point. The question we should be asking is this: Does my small group have an inward focus or an outward focus?

Outwardly focused groups seek to engage the world. They are aware of what is happening in their congregation and in the broader community that surrounds them. They make it a priority to serve people in need, sometimes to the point of keeping in touch with international missionaries and the like.

Inwardly focused groups are just the opposite. They view their small group as a way to huddle against the world—although they think of it in terms of building existing relationships within the group. This sounds good in theory, but more often than not the group ends up breaking apart due to interpersonal conflict.

In other words, outwardly focused groups are vibrant, healthy and growing. Inwardly focused groups are protective, territorial and dying.

Unfortunately, there usually isn't a lot of middle ground between the two. I think of what Big Tom Callahan says in the movie *Tommy Boy*: "When it comes to auto parts, son, you're either growin' or you're dyin'. There ain't no third direction." The same is true when it comes to most facets of spiritual growth and transformation, including small groups.

Moving Outward

Right about now you might be thinking, *I'm going to make sure my small group has an outward focus.* And I hope it does. But groups rarely become outwardly or inwardly focused as a result of some arbitrary choice. Nobody would consciously choose to set up a selfish, dying small group—would they?

No, the path to becoming inwardly or outwardly focused is more complicated than a single choice, and it is always centered on obedience.

After all, any productive small group will be regularly exposed to the commands of God through the Bible, the Holy Spirit and the witness of other Christians. Those commands include things like "love your neighbor as yourself," "make disciples of all nations," "give generously," and "look after orphans and widows in their distress."

Groups that consistently obey these commands (and the others like it) become outwardly focused. Groups that consistently ignore these commands become inwardly focused. It really is that simple.

That being the case, here are a few tips to help your group make obedience and application a high priority:

- *Get it on the calendar.* As a group leader, the best thing you can do when it comes to application is proactively lead your group members into situations that allow them to obey what they have learned. This can include service projects, mission trips, prayer walks, evangelistic opportunities and anything else you can think of. Get some events on everyone's calendar and make it clear that application is an "official" part of your small group.

  Actually, you don't have to take the lead on this by yourself. If there is another person in the group who shows an affinity for doing something tangible to obey God's commands, consider making him or her the "application champion" for the group (or whatever title works best). Empower that person to regularly present to the group opportunities for obedience and to assist you in the administration of those opportunities.

- *Desegregate application in your group meetings.* Too many small group studies contain an application section at the end of each session's material. This is usually a one-sentence piece of encouragement based on the topic covered during the discussion—"Look for ways to love your neighbors as you go about your life this week." Bah! Why separate application from the rest of your group's time together?

As an alternative, keep a sharp eye out for biblical commands and outward principles during every part of your group meeting. And when you see one, highlight it for your group and start a conversation about practical obedience right then and there. For example: "All right, it's pretty clear that Jesus is commanding us to visit people who are in prison. How can we make that happen as a group in the next couple of weeks?"

- *Make accountability part of the conversation.* What if you asked an accountability question each time your group got together? Like: "Last week we talked about the importance of regularly submitting to God's Word. So, how many of us read the Bible at least five times this week?" The goal of a question like that is not to embarrass anyone or be judgmental. Rather, it sends the message that obedience is the expected reaction to God's commands.

- *Use positive reinforcement.* One of the best ways to prevent accountability from becoming judgmental is to regularly celebrate the times when group members obey and apply God's Word. This can range from a simple acknowledgment—"I'm really proud of you, Jennifer"—to a literal party where you highlight the progress made by everyone in the group.

I can't think of a better way to close out this section than the way I began this chapter: "Do not merely listen to the word, and so deceive yourselves. Do what it says."

Why Bother?

As I move toward the end of writing this book, it strikes me that those reading it may be grappling with some difficult questions: *Why should I bother with any of this? Why should I lead a small group at all?*

Those are questions I've asked myself. In ten years of leading small groups, my wife and I have had three or four serious conversations about whether we would continue as group leaders—even if we would continue as group members. And the conclusions that Jess and I reached on those occasions are the best answers I can give as to why anyone should lead a group.

Whether continuing or just starting out, you should lead a small group because in doing so you will contribute to the kingdom of God. You will grow spiritually. You will help others grow spiritually. You will have fun. You will give yourself a chance to form deep, life-changing friendships. You will contribute to others forming deep, life-changing friendships. You will learn new things about God and his Word. You will learn new things about yourself. You will help others learn new things and apply them in ways that compound everything I've just mentioned. And you will be obeying God.

My wife and I have been married for more than eight years, and in that time we've had the privilege of connecting with more than one hundred individuals through the ministry of small groups. We've seen marriages begin and end. We've seen children burst into the world and flourish. We've seen members of our groups serve the local church in dozens of ways—including starting small groups of their own. We've also seen members of our groups serve as missionaries in places like Haiti and Israel and inner-city Chicago.

I want to be clear: Jess and I are not responsible for any of this. We have tried to be good stewards of things like time and money and houses. We have committed to serving the members of our groups out of obedience to God, and in the meantime we have been blessed a hundredfold as a result of those investments.

The story of your group (or groups) will be different from what

I've experienced—at least in the particular details of who, what, when and where. But I'm confident the ending will be the same: You will glorify God with your faithful and obedient service, and you will be blessed.

Appendix 1

Further Resources on SmallGroups.com

SmallGroups.com is the largest online archive of resources for churches and small group leaders. Here are some of the best tools available specifically for group leaders.

Basic Training

Articles

- "How to Host a Small-Group Meeting" by Randall Neighbor
- "Seven Mistakes of New Small Group Leaders" by Reid Smith
- "The Friends of a Group Leader" by Heather Zempel
- "The Three Levels of Small Group Problems" by Heather Zempel
- "This Is Why They Call You a 'Leader'" by Sam O'Neal

Downloadable Resources

- Evaluations for Small Group Leaders
- Foundations of a Small Group Leader
- How to Prepare for a Bible Study
- Making Small Groups Fun
- Small Group Host Orientation Guide
- Small Group Leader Orientation Guide

Starting a Small Group

Articles

- "Cutting the Cord" by Eric Metcalf
- "Starting Right" by Mike Mack
- "Successfully Launching a Small Group" by Reid Smith

Downloadable Resources

- Reviving a Dying Small Group
- Small Group Member Orientation Guide
- Starting a New Small Group (E-Training)

Recruiting Group Members

Articles

- "Get Your Groups Noticed!" by Alan Danielson
- "Small Group Advertising" by Tom Bandy
- "Start, Fill, and Keep" by Alan Danielson

Downloadable Resources

- Creating Video Ads and Testimonies
- Small Group Assimilation Strategies

Choosing and Writing Curriculum

Articles

- "Do-It-Yourself Video Curriculum" by Alan Danielson
- "Five Types of Questions" by Mac Lake
- "What Makes a Good Bible Study?" by JoHannah Reardon
- "What Should Our Group Study?" by Spence Shelton

Downloadable Resources

- Choosing and Evaluating Bible Studies
- Making Bible Study Transformational (E-Training)

Leading Discussion in a Small Group

Articles

- "Evaluating Group Discussions" by JoHannah Reardon (assessment)
- "Fighting Heresy in Churches and Small Groups" by J. I. Packer
- "How to Ask Stimulating Discussion Questions" by Joel Comiskey
- "How to Stimulate Better Discussions" by Mark Howell
- "Permission to Be Real" by Seth Widner
- "Writing Questions That Spark Discussion" by Rick Lowry

Downloadable Resources

- Discussing Doctrine and Theology
- Small Group Facilitator Orientation Guide

Prayer and Worship

Articles

- "An Audience of One" by Andrew Wheeler
- "A Theology of Small-Group Worship" by Bonnie McMaken
- "How to Pray for Another Group Member" by Randall Neighbor
- "How to Pray for One Another" by Andrew Wheeler
- "Worship in Small Groups" by Joel Comiskey

Downloadable Resources

- Evaluating Prayer in Your Small Group
- Meaningful Worship in Small Groups
- Revolutionary Prayer in Your Small Group

Group Dynamics

Articles

- "Avoiding Pitfalls in Group Dynamics" by Reid Smith
- "Facing Shame Issues in a Small Group" by Mark Bonham
- "No More Mr. Nice Group" by John Ortberg
- "On the Clock" by Reid Smith
- "When Group Members Don't Show Up" by Allen White

Downloadable Resources
- Becoming a Great Listener
- Hospitality in Small Groups

Building Relationships

Articles
- "Making Relational Deposits" by Dan Lentz
- "Permission to Be Real" by Seth Widner
- "The Benefits of Transparency" by Terry Powell
- "Understanding the Connecting Continuum" by Bill Search

Downloadable Resources
- Creating Community
- Effective Intergenerational Small Groups

Handling Conflict

Articles
- "A Time to Fight" by Bill Donahue
- "Avoiding Pitfalls in Group Dynamics" by Reid Smith
- "Engaging Conflict in Small Groups" by Mark Bonham
- "Loving Those You Disagree With" by James Bryan Smith
- "The Hidden Danger of Broken Relationships" by Wayne Cordeiro
- "When Children Behave Badly" by Rachel Gilmore

Downloadable Resources
- Dealing with Divorce in Your Small Group
- Handling Conflict in Small Groups
- Ministering to Difficult Group Members

Men and Women

Articles
- "Drawing Men into Small Groups" by Patrick Morley
- "The Common Obstacles Men Face in Groups" by Dave Treat

- "Why Some Women Resist Community" by Nancy Barton

Downloadable Resources
- Effective Small Groups for Men
- Effective Small Groups for Women
- Family-Friendly Small Groups
- Life-Changing Small Groups for Couples

Spiritual Growth

Articles
- "Fessing Up" by Gordon T. Smith
- "Looking for Life-Change" by Jenn Peppers and Tara Miller
- "On Spiritual Direction" by Eugene Peterson
- "The Truth About Transformation" by Dan Lentz

Downloadable Resources
- Finding Focus Through Spiritual Disciplines
- Leading a Life-Changing Bible Study
- Soul Care
- Spiritual Disciplines for Busy Church Leaders

Multiplication and Numerical Growth

Articles
- "Branching Over Birthing" by Reid Smith
- "Cell Biology for the Church" by Bill Tenny-Brittian
- "The 'Joys' of Multiplication" by Randy Frazee
- "Three Ways to Birth a New Small Group" by Dave Earley
- "Why Dividing Small Groups Is a Dumb Idea" by Larry Osborne
- "You Can't Have Babies If You Don't Get Pregnant" by Dave Earley

Downloadable Resources
- Grow the Number of Small Groups in Your Church
- Growing Small Groups

Mission

Articles

- "Organic Small Groups" by Joe Myers
- "Small Groups and the Missional Renaissance" by Reggie McNeal
- "Small Groups and the Mission of God" by Alan Hirsch
- "Taking the Next Step to Serve" by Keri Wyatt Kent
- "Why Small Groups Need to Be on Mission" by Alan Danielson

Downloadable Resources

- Missional Small Groups
- Planning a Group Service Project
- Planning a Short-Term Missions Trip as a Group
- Small Groups and Evangelism

Appendix 2

Sample Icebreakers

Each of these icebreakers was originally written by Sam O'Neal for SmallGroups.com.

A Construction Contest

Purpose: To get people thinking about the importance of a foundation.

Activity: Before starting this activity, you'll need to gather a large supply of building materials. These could be actual blocks or Legos, or you could just use pillows and shoes and other items lying around the house. When the members of your group or class arrive, arrange them into separate teams of four to five people.

The goal of this activity is for each team to build a structure using the materials you provide. It can be any kind of structure the team chooses—the only rules are that it must be resting on the floor, and it must be freestanding (nothing holding it up). The team with the tallest structure after five minutes of building will be declared the winner.

Unpacking Questions

- Have everyone examine the winning structure. What was the key to the winning team's success?

- Was there anything exceptional about the winning structure that allowed it to go higher?

Don't Say "The"

Purpose: To help group members think about the words we say.

Activity: In this activity have your group or class divide into smaller groups of two or three people, then ask them to work through the following discussion questions. Whenever you say "Switch," they need to break up the smaller groups and join other people to continue the conversation.

There is just one catch: they are forbidden to say the word *the*. If they mess up, they will need to give themselves one point for every time they say *the*. At the end of five minutes or so, the person with the fewest amount of points will be declared the winner.

Questions

- What parts of your week were fun?
- What parts of your week were hard?
- What hilarious jokes have you heard this month?
- What meal did you enjoy most this month?
- What TV show have you enjoyed most this year?

Unpacking Questions

- Was it hard to control your tongue in that way? What caused you to slip and let *the* come out?
- Without mentioning names, what is the most hurtful thing anyone has ever said to you? What is the kindest thing anyone has said?
- Why are those memories still strong in your mind?

Drawing Your Fears

Purpose: To help people start thinking about the topic of fear.

Activity: Give each group member a blank sheet of paper and a few crayons or colored pencils. Ask them to spend five minutes or so drawing a picture that symbolizes one of their biggest fears as a child. This could be something specific (like a particular monster) or it could be something more abstract (like the thought of parents divorcing).

After the time is up, ask for volunteers to share their drawings and explain what the drawings represent. Allow time for anyone who wants to share, but don't force anyone who is unwilling to volunteer.

Unpacking Questions

• Were there any similarities between our childhood fears—any themes or common elements that popped up repeatedly?

• What comes to your mind when you think of fearing God? Where did you get that idea?

• How is the fear of God different from the fear represented by our drawings? What are some of the problems that occur when we talk about fearing God?

Out in the Dark

Purpose: To help group members experience a sense of injustice and separation.

Activity: Split your group into two sections, then announce that you would like each section to brainstorm an answer to this question: What is the difference between justice and injustice?

Have one of the groups remain in your normal meeting location (including comfortable chairs and snacks), but ask the other group to discuss the question outside. Do not provide any chairs or food, but encourage them to leave as they are and discuss the issue outside in the dark. (If it is daytime, or if there is inclement weather, ask the second group to brainstorm in a smaller room with the lights turned off.)

After five to ten minutes, bring the groups back together and ask the following debriefing questions.

Unpacking Questions

- What did your group decide is the difference between justice and injustice? (Leader's note: If one of the members of the "outside" group grumbles here about experiencing injustice, that is great. Ask them to explain what they mean, and then continue with the following questions.)

- For those in the "outside" group, how did it change your experience to be brainstorming in the dark?

- How did it change your experience to know that the other group was inside with comfortable chairs and snacks?

- For those of the "inside" group, were you concerned about the people outside? For how long did that concern stay in the front of your mind?

The World on Our Backs

Purpose: To help group members begin thinking internationally and missionally.

Activity: Instruct your group members to examine their various items of clothing and identify what countries they were manufactured in. (People will probably need to help each other read tags in order to accomplish this, so let them know that doing so is acceptable.)

After several minutes have passed, have group members who are willing share which countries their clothes have come from. If time allows, encourage everyone to pray briefly for God's guidance for those countries and for the individuals who had a hand in manufacturing their clothes.

Unpacking Questions

- Were you surprised by the countries that were identified?

- Which country was farthest away?
- What responsibility (if any) do we have toward Christians and non-Christians in distant countries?

Notes

[1]Janet Kornblum, "Study: 25% of Americans Have No One to Confide In," *USA Today,* June 22, 2006.

[2]For example, see Reid Smith, "What Is the Ideal Size for a Small Group?" SmallGroups.com, August 9, 2008, www.smallgroups.com/discussion/questionanswer/reidsmith/q2.html.

[3]Eugene Peterson, *Eat This Book* (Grand Rapids: Eerdmans, 2006).

[4]Will Miller and Glenn Sparks, *Refrigerator Rights* (New York: Penguin Putnam, 2002).

[5]Will Miller, "What Are Refrigerator Rights?" *Refrigerator Rights,* November 2, 2006, www.fridgerights.blogspot.com.

[6]Stephanie Voiland, "The Theology of Huckleberry Pie," from the Small Groups.com training resource "Hospitality in Your Small Group."

[7]Jim Egli, "A Small Group Leader's Most Important Job," SmallGroups.com, February 15, 2010, www.smallgroups.com/articles/2010/sgleadersmost importantjob.html.

[8]Ibid.

[9]Randall Neighbor, "How to Host a Small-Group Meeting," SmallGroups .com, March 12, 2008, www.smallgroups.com/articles/2008/howtohosta smallgroupmeeting.html.

[10]David Kolb's ELT model of learning styles is probably the best-known system; see his book *Experiential Learning: Experience as the Source of Learning and Development* (Upper Saddle River, N.J.: Prentice Hall, 1984). Other models are explained and evaluated in Robert Sternberg's book *Thinking Styles* (New York: Cambridge University Press, 1999).

[11]For more information on the VARK model, see Neil Fleming, *Teaching and Learning Styles: VARK Strategies* (Christchurch, N.Z.: Neil Fleming, 2006);

and *VARK: A Guide to Learning Styles,* 2010, www.vark-learn.com.

[12]Names have been changed for any people referenced in my current or former small groups.

[13]Fleming, *Teaching and Learning Styles.*

[14]I first heard the phrase "idiot question" from Larry Osborne in the "Small Groups Starter Kit" produced by North Coast Church in 2008.

[15]Many of these ideas were adapted from the infographic by Sam O'Neal, "Small Groups Feng Shui," *Small Groups Digizine,* Fall 2010.

[16]Andrew Wheeler, *Together in Prayer* (Downers Grove, Ill.: InterVarsity Press, 2009), p. 39.

[17]Mark Bonham, "Engaging Conflict in Small Groups," SmallGroups.com, August 6, 2008, www.smallgroups.com/articles/2008/engagingconflictin smallgroups.html.

[18]Excerpted from "Statement of Faith," National Association of Evangelicals, www.nae.net/about-us/statement-of-faith.